"Paul's new book weaves together an intricate pattern regarding the crisis of faith within the Catholic Church and establishes necessary steps in restoring in the minds of the faithful what it truly means to be Catholic."

Michael Hichborn

Founder and president of the Lepanto Institute

As in his previous work, *Christians Must Reunite: Now Is the Time,* here again, Paul A. Nelson shares with us his gift of succinctly diagnosing the malady and presenting the remedy.

The deconstruction of Catholic tradition, beauty, faith, and truth did not happen overnight. It was a gradual process which led to many—if not most—Catholics not believing that the Holy Eucharist is truly the person of Jesus Christ. If it truly is not Jesus, then reverence does not matter. If it truly is not Jesus, then the power of COVID-19 is greater than the power of the Sacraments, and the centrality of government is more important than the centrality of Christ and His sacrifice.

This is a must-read book because it demonstrates that the call to love our enemy is not antithetical to knowing who our enemies are and what they have done. *Restoring Our Catholic Identity* explains what we need to do to restore our Church.

David L. Gray

Catholic author/theologian, and radio host on the Guadalupe Radio Network

Restoring Our Catholic Identity

Paul A. Nelson

LEONINE PUBLISHERS
PHOENIX, ARIZONA

Published by Leonine Publishers LLC
Phoenix, Arizona
USA

ISBN-13: 978-1-942190-65-3
Library of Congress Control Number: 2021916921
10 9 8 7 6 5 4 3 2 1

Visit us online at www.leoninepublishers.com
For more information: info@leoninepublishers.com

Dedicated to

Our Lord Jesus Christ,

and my grandchildren:
Sean, Brooke, Leigh, Emma, Bryce, Hailey, and Brady.

I love them all dearly.

Contents

Foreword

The church Paul Nelson and his wife visited in Richmond, Virginia, never quite left his mind. It was as unsightly as any building he had ever seen—but it wasn't just a building, it was a Roman Catholic Church, where he would soon receive the Body of Christ on his tongue. When he genuflected toward the altar, he found no tabernacle. Thereafter, even from the altar, he felt an absence all around. Rather than being pulled into something majestic and liturgically beautiful, the Nelsons were staggered by the church's sterility and *absence*. It was as if the "Catholic community" had made a purposeful attempt to contracept and mock two thousand years of resplendence.

When Nelson approached a deacon afterward to challenge him on the parish's "Catholic-less" church, he was told, among other things, *"We kind of do our own thing."*

And that, of course, is *the* problem. The deacon's casual statement is indicative of the disease Paul Nelson cogently points out in his latest work, *Restoring Our Catholic Identity*. Nelson is refreshingly blunt and precisely on target with what he knows is leading to the piecemeal ruination of the Catholic Church. Nelson, a revert and wise Catholic voice, has long seen a desacralization of what saints, mystics, martyrs, and countless millions of worshippers have been devoted to down through the millennia. Rather than running from the bleakness of the days, Nelson has chosen to shine his light directly upon it. The reader will be thankful that he has.

In a compelling, step-by-step fashion, the author lays out the hydra-like plagues of today's post-Vatican II Church: Eucharist in the hand, shacking-up young Catholics, effeminate priests, Richard Rohr-like thinkers, bland preaching, wrong-headed charismatic activities, a cold-shouldering of the Church's patrimony, wayward Church-wide movements, and socialistic ideologies. The list, sadly, goes on—but Nelson doesn't miss a single corruption.

In *Restoring Our Catholic Identity*, Nelson joins with countless intentional Catholics who regard the malformations in the Mass, clergy tepidity, and looseness with the moral teachings and practice of the faith as the corrosive items causing Catholics to line up on a gangplank in the middle of a roiling sea. Nelson understands a bleak fact: Generations of strong Catholic families die each day in America because rather than being led to sanctity, devoted worship of Christ, and veneration of Mary and the saints, Catholics are being led to a certain worship of themselves. Nelson knows that too many modern priests today skip right past speaking of sin. The road has widened for Catholics, not narrowed.

Intentional Catholics, perhaps naively, once thought that the unsightly movements within the Church would—one by one—just begin to disappear. Instead, the opposite has occurred. The diseases resulting from the scourge of Modernism have crawled into the unsteady Barque of St. Peter. This sturdy two-thousand-year-old vessel, at times, seems just about ready to sink—and Nelson tells the reader why.

A staggering number of Catholics do not believe in the Real Presence. Others refuse to go to the Sacrament of Confession. Countless other Catholics rarely attend Mass, and some

have opted to stop altogether. Rosaries, fasting, and litanies—
the majority of Catholics believe today—were for an earlier
black-and-white generation. While vice president, Joe Biden
officiated the "marriage" of two men, and he has publicly stated
that children should be able to determine their own gender. His
strong advocacy for abortion is diabolical. Biden is a Catholic.
Throughout the run-up to the 2020 presidential election, few
bishops have even whispered a contrary thought—let alone
condemnation—regarding his anti-Catholic views. Cardinal
Wilton Gregory, from the Archdiocese of Washington, has
already publicly stated that he will not hesitate to give Biden
Holy Communion.

What to do?

Paul Nelson knows: First, lay out how and when these
deviations from the faith took root; and thereafter, explain precisely and historically why they have no place in the Church.
Noble-hearted saints and reformers, Nelson says, are what is
most necessary now. At the end of *Restoring Our Catholic Identity*, he refers us to many of the very holy ones who understood
how to address and overcome the grave problems Catholics
faced in their time, encouraging us to do the same. Nelson gives
us great hope.

It is a time now for the purification of souls, sacristies,
sinners, and of course the hemorrhaging Church. Read Paul
Nelson's work, and you'll understand what has led the Church
to her crucifixion—and what your part might be in helping to
remove it from its cross.

Kevin Wells

Author of *The Priests We Need to Save the Church*

Introduction

As I sit down to begin writing this book, it occurs to me that we in the USA—and indeed the whole world—are in the throes of a tremendous threat to humanity, and there is now a great struggle to maintain the way of life most of us have become accustomed to. The threat we now face is called COVID-19 (also known as the coronavirus).

The stock market has plummeted such that all of the profits/gains realized in the last three and a half years have been wiped out, and that only took a little over a week to happen. People are panicking and stockpiling food, and they are purchasing guns and ammunition like never before. For some strange reason, one of the most precious and sought-after items is toilet paper, of all things!

Unbelievably, most Catholic Masses have been suspended because of the federal and state mandate that no more than ten people can congregate at a time, for fear of passing on or catching the virus. Many people have already died from this strange new sickness, and from all indications there will be thousands—maybe millions—more. This is scary stuff indeed.

Regarding those around the world who have no faith, I can't imagine the horror they must be experiencing. The hopelessness they no doubt feel at the loss of their invested money, and everything else happening, must be almost unbearable. I sincerely wouldn't want to be in their shoes right now. I don't say that because I'm unaffected by what is happening; we're all going through this together, albeit maybe from a different perspective. I say it because my hope and faith is in Almighty God. As a Catholic Christian, I believe that what we possess in this world, including money, nice cars, prestigious jobs, or fame—and even our very lives—is not the most important thing, and it is only very temporary. The state of our souls is what really matters.

The important point I attempted to put forth in my last book, *Christians Must Reunite: Now is the Time*, was that all who believe in Jesus Christ and acknowledge what He did for us would be wise to return to the Catholic Church. When I made that plea, I was addressing weak Catholics, fallen-away Catholics, and all members of the 30,000-plus denominations of Protestants. In light of the situation in the world now, which has markedly worsened, "now is the time" takes on an even greater significance.

In this book, I will address the many problems existing in the Catholic Church, which have worsened and become more intense in the last half century. Along the way, I will propose ways to restore the true identity of the One, Holy, Catholic, and Apostolic Church. We must cease trying to make the Church something it was never meant to be. I contend that we should have never moved in the direction of Protestantism in an attempt to conform to the modern world. It should be the other way around: The world needs to conform to the teachings of the Church, which are and always have been immutable.

Even though the Church is somewhat wounded and broken, we know the gates of hell will never prevail against it. It remains the only Church founded by Jesus Christ Himself. We need to remember that, and the hierarchy and clergy ought to think twice about some of the so-called "innovations" they've come up with, in the name of ecumenism and a "new" evangelization. A reversal of these trends needs to happen if we are to reclaim our former sense of holiness and the unique nature of the Catholic Church in the world. We owe God no less.

Chapter 1
When the Church Changed

Imagine that a devout Catholic fell asleep in 1961 and was preserved in a time capsule until around late 1977, when he was awakened. Further imagine that newly revived person deciding that one of his greatest desires was to attend the Holy Sacrifice of the Mass, worship God, and receive the Holy Eucharist. What a disappointment and sense of shock that poor person would have experienced. The Church of Jesus Christ was transformed, seemingly, into something totally different.

That reawakened Catholic would have heard folk music instead of the beautiful and timeless hymns and chants he loved so much. The reverent way the faithful once approached—in their Sunday best—the altar rail, where they knelt down to receive the body, blood, soul and divinity of Our Lord directly from the priest, on the tongue, would have been replaced by another scenario. He would have seen people walking toward the altar—many in flip-flops and tee-shirts—and receiving Christ in their dirty hands, putting the Host in their mouths as they would a cookie or potato chip. Many of the faithful would receive the Eucharist from a layperson, called an Extraordinary Minister.

To add insult to injury, that poor reawakened individual would have been shocked and baffled to see that the priest now faced the congregation during the divine Liturgy, instead of the tabernacle behind the altar. In fact, he may also have realized that there was no tabernacle behind the altar; it was now put in a back room, called a "reservation chapel." The person in my made-up scenario would have undoubtedly been extremely sad- dened and disappointed to have witnessed such drastic changes in his beloved Church.

Now, due to the fact that these changes were forced on the faithful by the Church leadership, without their input, they could do nothing but acquiesce. Catholics who had learned and understood their faith well rebelled the best they could to these abuses and the extreme makeover of the Church they revered and loved so much. But their rebellion was ignored and discounted.

Why did all these changes occur? I will enumerate the ter- rible mistakes made by those in power during Vatican II.

Before that, I must make some statements that may not sit well with some—especially those who like the Church in its present state, and those who believe Catholics need to change with the times.

Long before Vatican II, there began an infiltration of the Catholic Church by many seeking the ruination of it altogether. Some of the infiltrators were communists, Freemasons, and homosexuals. A woman named Bella Dodd[1] was part of a com- munist cabal seeking to recruit communist and homosexual men who would be willing to enter seminaries, with the intent of becoming priests and bishops, so they could do as much damage and effect as much negative change as they could, in order to destroy the Catholic Church and achieve their sinister objectives. The Church was always the greatest enemy of evil and the communist movement that was trying to grab the world by the throat and control its people. About twelve years before the commencement of the Second Vatican Council, and after her return to the Church, Bella told her Catholic friend, Alice von Hildebrand, there were four cardinals that she knew of within the Vatican, who were active Communists.

When the aforementioned Bella Dodd came back to the Catholic Church of her youth, she was brought in by none other than future saint Archbishop Fulton J. Sheen. She freely admitted to many people that she, in fact, assisted in recruiting over 1,100 men into the Church, in order to destroy it from within. Now, we can reasonably assume that she wasn't the only one doing the recruiting, so one can only imagine how many more of these devious and presumably communist/homosexual men were placed in the Church seeking to destroy it. It's very chilling and disconcerting, to say the least.

Again, by the time Ms. Dodd testified before Congress, many of those infiltrators had become bishops, and even cardinals. From all indications, those bishops and cardinals gave special treatment to priests who did their bidding, letting them run seminaries, which spawned weak and misled priests, many of whom were later promoted to bishops themselves because they towed the line. It was clericalism at its worst, and good and holy priests and bishops were treated as second-class "citizens." The damage to the Church was exponential.

Freemason Infiltration

The infiltration of Freemasons into the Church is a very disturbing story, and many refuse to believe it, even in the face of stark evidence.

For the purpose of giving you, the reader, a general idea regarding how the Freemasons have attempted to undermine the Catholic Church, I will include some quotes from some excellent books on the subject. I strongly encourage you to acquire these writings and delve deeper into this subject.

The following words were written by Dr. Taylor R. Marshall in his extensive and eye-opening account of why the Catholic Church has drastically been transformed over the years, and he contends that it began way before the Second Vatican Council:

"Formally organized Freemasonry originated in 1717, two hundred years after the 1517 Reformation. It grew out of the anti-Catholicism, Deism, and rationalism of its time. Reason, not faith, was prized by this epoch, and the Freemasonic lodges proliferated. Organized religion was rejected in favor of sentiment that all religions are equally grasping for the unknown 'Great Architect of the Universe.' This is why the Freemason Benjamin Franklin tithed to all the religions and denominations in his day. This is also why Freemasons enshrine the scriptures of all religions on their altar: the Holy Bible, the Koran, the Vedas, the Zend-Avesta, the Sohar, the Kabbalah, the Bhagavad Gita, and the Upanishads. They are, for the Freemason, all equally true and all equally false. They are, for the Freemason, merely the kindergarten sketches of children picturing God....

"The Catholic Church excommunicated any Catholic who joined Freemasonry, because it is a religion of all religions. Although it is a secret Society, it makes no secret about seeking a new world order in which all religions are honored and treated as equally true. In its pursuit of equality, it also desires the equal distribution of human property."[2]

I will now quote the words of Bishop Athanasius Schnei-der, a very holy and highly respected prelate in the Catholic Church. This appears in the foreword to the aforementioned book by Taylor R. Marshall, and it certainly bears repeating:

"In the last sixty years, there has been a continuously growing hostility toward the Divine Person of Jesus Christ and His claim to be the sole Redeemer and Teacher of human-kind. This hostility of the allegedly 'nice,' 'tolerant,' 'optimistic' modern world expresses itself in slogans such as 'We don't want Christ to reign over us'; and 'We will never acknowledge a Church that will not unconditionally accept the mindset of the modern world.'

"This hostility has reached its peak in our day. Not a few high-ranking members of the Catholic Church's hierarchy have not only yielded to the relentless demands of the modern world; they are, with or without conviction, actively collaborating in the implementation of its principles in the daily life of the Church in all areas and on all levels.

"Many wonder how it could happen that the Church's doctrine, morals, and liturgy have been disfigured to such a large extent. How is it that there remains very little difference between the predominant spirit in the life of the Church in our days and the mindset of the modern world? The modern world, after all, is inspired by the principles of the French Revolution: the absolute freedom of man from any divine revelation or commandment; the absolute equality that abolishes not only any social or religious hierarchy but even differences between the sexes; and a brotherhood of many so uncritical that it even eliminates any distinction on the basis of religion...

"With devastation and confusion in the Church now in full public view, it is time to expose the historical roots and the perpetrators of this harm. It may help many in the Church to wake up out of their lethargy and to stop acting as if everything is just fine."[3]

Bishop Schneider expands on the subject of Freemasonry in his recent book, *Christus Vincit: Christ's Triumph Over the Darkness of the Age.* This work is done in a question and answer format, with the questions being asked by Diane Montagna, an esteemed American journalist based in Rome. I highly recommend reading it.

Ms. Montagna asked this question:

"Can you say more about the place Freemasonry occupies in the secularist movement?"

Bishop Schneider answered this way:

"Freemasonry is a movement which has philosophical connections with English Deism. As I said before, according to Deism, God has nothing to do with us, so we are completely free. This was in some way the mental premise for traditional Freemasons as we know them. At the same time, Freemasonry is a kind of religion—we cannot forget this. At the heart of Freemasonry is a religion, a cult, a worship."

Ms. Montagna further asked:

"Is it Satanism?"

Bishop Schneider replied:

"Alas, ultimately it is close to Satanism. Not every Freemasonic group is Satanic, but the roots are Satanic and lead to Satanism in the highest degrees of Freemasonry.

"Freemasonry is ultimately a Gnostic religion. Gnosticism was flourishing at the time of Our Lord Jesus Christ, precisely in the first and second centuries in the Greco-Roman world. This movement is characterized by the belief in imaginary intellectual entities, divorced from the evidence of concrete reality and denying a true, supernatural, and historically based divine revelation....

"The Freemasons took the main part of their thinking from historical Gnosticism."4

Just so the reader is clear, when a Catholic joins the Freemasons, he is immediately excommunicated. No, the Church never relented and changed its teaching on this subject. Just know this: The "Great Architect of the Universe" to which Freemasons refer is not the God we as Catholics worship.

David L. Gray, an excellent Catholic author and theologian, wrote an in-depth work, entitled, *The Catholic Catechism on Freemasonry*. His approach is from a theological perspective rather than an apologetic one. Mr. Gray is a convert to the Catholic religion, and he was once well ensconced in the network of Freemasonry. As he describes it, "I was raised to the Sublime Degree of Master Mason." He was only twenty-two years of age at the time. Over the next several years, he earned higher degrees within the Grand Lodge. Many honors were conferred upon him along the way.

It's important to note that David L. Gray was really an Agnostic while he was involved in Freemasonry. His conversion to Christianity is a stark reminder that Our Lord is always watching over every human being. I will quote David's words here because I think what he says is very chilling, but ultimately extremely uplifting:

"After spending my early adult life as a Deist and Agnostic, I came to definitely and unforgettably believe in the person of Jesus Christ in September of 2004. It happened that while I was in the process of trying to commit suicide by asphyxiation, I heard an audible voice that told me, 'I love you. I am here.' After soon realizing and accepting that it was, surprisingly, the voice of the Lord who I, heretofore, thought was the leading fictional character of a fraud religion, from that day forward, I committed to following Jesus, which eventually led me to being baptized a Protestant on August 28, 2005, and being confirmed into the Catholic Church on August 8, 2006, the Feast of Saint Dominic de Guzman."5

Mr. Gray went on to attain an undergraduate degree in theology from Franciscan University of Steubenville in Ohio, and he earned a master's degree in theology from Ohio Dominican University. I highly recommend reading *The Catholic Catechism on Freemasonry,* for a scholarly in-depth education on why Catholics cannot, under any circumstances, be involved with Freemasonry. As a man who knows the world of Freemasonry very well from actually being on the inside, Mr. Gray instructs us that it is really a religion akin to Protestantism. He quotes extensively from papal documents, canon law, and documents emanating from the Congregation for the Doctrine of the Faith. Interestingly, he states this regarding the approach he takes in his book:

"I avoid, as often as possible, any reference to Masonic scholars, simply because the diversity of their opinions in regards to the ritual, allegory, and symbolism of Freemasonry does not add any weight whatsoever to the argument that is being made. Quoting what one scholar of Freemasonry has said about a topic is like quoting what one Protestant scholar has said about a topic. For, they all disagree with one another and none of them have a deposit of faith or a definitive source of authority to draw from."[6]

Ecumenism

For some reason, there is a mistaken belief on the part of many Catholics these days that Protestants and Catholics can worship together; we can attend their "meetings/services," and they can attend our Holy Mass. After all, they say, we all believe in the same God; we should all be nice and get along in the spirit of ecumenism. Why do modern-day Catholics believe actions like this are now very acceptable? In my opinion, the main reason is a severe lack of proper catechesis. Ignorance of all things actually Catholic is pervasive among the faithful. The good news is that this situation is correctable, but bishops and priests need to get onboard and start changing some things.

Can they reverse this damage and the misguided idea that being ecumenical and promoting the idea that all religions are equal is a worthy goal for all Catholics around the world? And, yes, we Catholics should always be gracious and should interact with our separated brethren. But many have seriously lost sight of the fact that our primary responsibility as Christians belonging to the very Church Jesus founded is to, "Go, therefore, and make disciples of all nations, baptizing them in the name of the Father, and of the Son, and of the Holy Spirit, teaching them to observe all that I have commanded you. And behold, I am with you always, until the end of the age" (Matthew 28:19-20).

To be sure, as Catholics, it's our job to evangelize those not in communion with our One, Holy, Catholic, and Apostolic Church, to gently help them to join our ranks. Since Vatican II, our leaders have instead made a tremendous effort to weaken our Catholic teaching and forsake most of the rich, beautiful things that have always distinguished us from those who are separated from the true Church. The result of this debacle is that we have lost our unique identity and are considered just another "denomination" out of the tens of thousands that exist.

In the short fifty-five years since the close of the Second Vatican Council, we have managed to make our Liturgy more Protestant-like; allowed our Catholic schools to be run by lay-people, who employ secular teachers who don't know or teach the faith; devastated our Catholic universities, allowing all kinds of non-Christian activities to take place on their campuses; redesigned and stripped down our Church buildings to the point where even many Protestant churches look more Catholic than ours; and allowed Catholics to participate in programs and actions that had always been frowned upon, and even forbidden.

All of this was allowed in an effort to take the Church in a different direction. Many "progressives" within the Church felt that we remained in "the dark ages," and that we needed to do these things to be relevant and conform to the secular winds blowing in the world. In my opinion—I'm not alone in this opinion—we have totally lost our identity. Instead of the sadly misled Protestants, and those of other man-made religions, being urged to come into the true Church, our leaders have managed to eviscerate what was once a meaningful, beautiful, and spiritual testament to Our Lord, including the way we worship.

It is now up to the good and holy bishops and priests, and the faithful laity, to stop this nonsense and turn things around. As I stated in my last book, all Catholics need to recommit to studying their faith, realizing that it is our solemn responsibility to do so. We as the laity also have responsibilities.

The Venerable Archbishop Fulton J. Sheen said it this way:

"Who's going to save our Church? It's not our bishops, it's not our priests and it is not the religious. It is up to you, the people. You have the minds, the eyes and the ears to save the Church. Your mission is to see that the priests act like priests, your bishops act like bishops, and the religious act like religious."

When we who know the teachings of the Church witness something in our parishes that is not in accord with our Church, it is incumbent upon us—indeed our obligation—to broach the subject with our pastor, make our objections known and explain why. Do your research on the subject so that you will know how to present your case intelligently. If you approach your pastor with respect and reverence, you should be received graciously.

One of the unfortunate things that came from the "spirit of Vatican II" was the institution of parish councils, which was an effort to make decisions on behalf of the parishes appear democratic. First of all, the Church is not a democracy and never has been. We are to follow the teachings and guidelines of the Church, which are never-changing. Now, parish councils should only weigh in on innocuous things that don't involve dogma and what should be presented to parishioners in the way of teaching, or the Liturgy; but that line has been crossed repeatedly around this country. Many times, these councils are populated with people who wield influence because of their ability to donate more money, or because of cliques that form. For the most part, they are allowed to control far too many things that occur within a parish community. The parish councils also need to be held in check by other members of the church, who should also get to contribute to what goes on in their parishes. But in matters of catechesis, the Liturgy, and all other matters of extreme importance, the pastor should be the go-to person and the final arbiter.

Chapter 2
The Post-Vatican II Church

The Second Vatican Council took place from 1962 until 1965. Even though this council of the Catholic Church's pope, cardinals, and bishops was reportedly a pastoral one that would not change existing doctrine, and it was to call upon the faithful to honor their baptism and confirmation and live as true Christians, it seems there was an underlying agenda by many liberal Church leaders to reshape, or transform, many aspects of the Church. Following the Council, instead of promoting a spiritual renewal of the faithful, an unbelievable stream of changes began to take place, which confused and angered millions of people. Of course, many also welcomed the fact that the Church was finally "coming into the modern world." It turned out that the next several decades would be a transformative time in the history of the Holy Roman Catholic Church.

The questions we must ask ourselves now are important, including:

Were those changes good for the souls of the faithful?

Did those changes enhance the spiritual lives of the faithful?

Did those changes bring more people into the Catholic Church, or did they cause a huge exodus from the Church?

Did more holy and faithful young men decide to enter the priesthood?

Have the myriad changes in the way the Catholic Church presents itself to the souls in its care increased their faith, bringing them closer to God?

Have the immutable teachings of the Church been watered down and sugarcoated so as to become more acceptable in the modern world?

You see, these are all-important questions we must begin to revisit, because we are living in perilous times. My contention is that we as a Church have made several devastating and grave errors in the name of trying to fit into the modern world. In many ways, we have moved in the wrong direction to satisfy those who never understood the Church in the first place. Unbeknownst to many otherwise faithful Catholics, they have been led into detrimental actions, believing that since bishops and priests had deemed something to be acceptable, it must be a good thing.

The attitudes and beliefs among bishops and priests vary widely. Many are just fine with the very liberal and modern changes that have been made, and many others are vehemently opposed to them. Much blame must be put on the terrible seminaries that many of them attended. Generally, young priests are heavily influenced by their instructors in those seminaries and also the pastors they work with when they leave the seminary and become parochial vicars. Priests entering into their new ministries would do well to read up on the Fathers of the Church and the saints. If something they learned in the seminary or heard from their pastors doesn't sit well with them, they need to do further research about it. When something is occurring at their parish that doesn't seem in line with Church teaching, it is incumbent upon them to approach the pastor and question it. I do realize that obedience is expected, so approaching the pastor with respect and reverence is important. If they are summarily dismissed or overruled, at least they tried to do the right thing. They must rely heavily on the Holy Spirit to guide them. The concept of "fraternal correction," which is taught by the Church, requires the clergy to gently question and correct a brother for anything being done that is not in step with the constant teachings of Jesus Christ. To remain silent is not an option when they become aware of a grave wrong; in fact, it is a sin.

In the following chapters, I will talk about what I and many others believe to be serious errors, mistakes in judgment, and downright malicious intent in some cases. At the present time, it is hard to distinguish the difference between a Catholic Church and a Protestant church. And as we have been recently informed by Pew Research,[1] only 31 percent of church-going Catholics in the United States actually believe in the Real Presence of Christ in the Eucharist. That is a direct result of the extremely poor catechesis and the loss of supernatural faith at the parishes around this country, and indeed the world.

Changes in the Mass

Before Vatican II, the Holy Sacrifice of the Mass was said in Latin (also known as the Tridentine Mass). As history records, Pope Saint Gregory (AD 590- 604) made slight changes to the Roman Missal, but he remained faithful to Tradition, only tweaking small, insignificant items. The Tridentine Mass was codified into Church Law in the year 1570, following the Council of Trent (1545- 1563). The Liturgy was essentially left untouched under the watchful eye of Pope Saint Pius V (1566-1572), except for minor, inconsequential adjustments; and it remained closely aligned with the Order of the Mass established by Pope Saint Gregory the Great.

Consequently, for roughly 1,300 years, the Catholic Mass remained virtually the same. And then came the Second Vatican Council. This council included several cardinals and bishops whose main purpose was to tear down what the Church had developed from its beginning, and build something altogether new, something the whole world would "love"; it would be a "nicer" version of the Catholic Church, which they believed would be welcoming to all human beings. It seems that their conclusion was that if they avoided the very hard teachings of the Church and watered down many of the other ones, it could advance the belief among the faithful that all Christian "denominations" are very similar; we could also play guitars during Mass and sing uplifting folk songs, forsaking the timeless, centuries-old, beautiful hymns and chants of old.

Could this huge effort on their part have been the fruits of the aforementioned infiltration of fake bishops and priests that had been taking place for decades leading up to this opportune period of time? Was this the "perfect storm" where these apostates would take charge in an unprecedented, non-supernatural coup attempt of Our Lord's Church? They were very successful in achieving most of their objectives, and we, the members of the Church, are still suffering the effects of what these deluded men did.

I call them "deluded" because they were deceived into thinking they were completely successful in what they did. They were the victims of instigations by the evil one for actually believing they could bring down Christ's Church. They made major changes in the Order of the Mass, and they were sin-gle-handedly responsible for the lack of good and holy men entering the priesthood, the closure of parishes worldwide, the weak catechesis and "nice" homilies that would come from priests, and so many other negatives that still exist in the Church today.

But changing the Latin Mass into an English-spoken Mass (or whatever other language), and having the priest face the people instead of the tabernacle, and instructing priests to avoid the hard teachings in their homilies, and everything else they did, DOES NOT change the fact that the faithful can still receive Our Lord's body, blood, soul and divinity in the Eucharist at every Mass. So, in the long run, have they succeeded in defeating Christ? Not in the least. I think it's about time to discuss how we can take many of these lost things back and restore our Catholic identity, thereby strengthening the faith of every Catholic. But it is going to take a Herculean effort on the part of all good and holy bishops and priests, but also the faithful laity. The obedient bishops and priests need to stop covering up for and apologizing for the bad ones. Biting their tongues when they see wrongdoing has to stop. Otherwise, they become complicit. And when I say "obedient," I mean obedient to Christ. In the final analysis, that is what really matters. Remember: fraternal correction.

What are some of the changes that have caused us to lose our Catholic identity? If we have the will to revisit these mis-guided modifications to our wonderful Church, we can restore our true Catholic identity.

Chapter 3
New Age Catholicism

A famous Trappist monk, Thomas Merton, converted to the Catholic faith in the 1940s. But many say he was never really all-in regarding the faith. He wrote an autobiography he called *The Seven Storey Mountain* in 1948, which was about his conversion. He went on to write many books over the years. He eventually became very interested in Asian forms of worship and Eastern mysticism and meditation. He left the Catholic "reservation," so-to-speak, when he dove headlong into other religious "worship" techniques. It is probably safe to say that Thomas Merton led the way for what was about to get the attention of other clergy members who obviously didn't think being authentically Catholic was enough, and that we needed some new "gimmicks."

Thomas Merton was probably heavily influenced by the strange ideas of Pierre Teilhard de Chardin, a Jesuit priest who believed in a so-called "Omega Point," or a level of consciousness to which the universe was evolving. Chardin's ideas were criticized and condemned by the Congregation for the Doctrine of the Faith repeatedly. In later years, many bishops of the Church spoke positively of many of Chardin's writings. Nonetheless, there was much error and heresy sprinkled throughout his ideas, which would lead some future priests and bishops into thinking they could alter Catholic thinking.

Some of the New Agers began to promote the idea that the world was overpopulated; that a man-made utopia was possible on earth if only we all followed their lead; and that there really is no sin, and we human beings have it within ourselves (because we are gods) to improve things in this world.

Many Catholic clergy were, unbelievably, caught up in all of this crazy mumbo-jumbo, and they were left unimpeded in passing it on to the easily influenced faithful. Today, many of the concepts that came from the New Age movement are still being foisted on the Catholics in the pews. These diabolical diversions and tactics lead people away from God and promote what has been dubbed a "Cosmic Christ." They focus on the so-called "god within"; whereas, essentially, New Agers worship themselves, instead of the true God of Salvation. We will explore this further.

Centering Prayer

In the late 1960s, a fascination with Transcendental Meditation was all the rage. Rock stars and entertainers were beginning to follow Eastern "mystics," like Maharishi Mahesh Yogi, and others, who worshipped Sri Krishna, the supreme god, in an effort to achieve the ultimate enlightenment. Disturbingly, some in the Catholic world got caught up in all this. I have already mentioned Trappist monk Thomas Merton's fascination with Eastern mysticism and meditation. Well, also during this time period, an impressionable Trappist abbot by the name of Thomas Keating started delving into this area. He and his brother monks began studying and learning some Hindu and

Buddhist meditation techniques; in straight language, they were practicing Transcendental Meditation. These priests were given week-long retreats by a Zen master.

Unfortunately, the Catholic monks were enamored and fell all-in with these Eastern meditation techniques. The only problem was that these actions were not Catholic in any way, shape, or form. They were in a quandary. They desperately wanted to find a way to present these teachings to Catholics, but it couldn't be done in the way they had learned it. It would never be allowed or accepted.

Father Keating teamed up with two other priests, Father M. Basil Pennington and Father William Meninger, and concocted a devious way of presenting these meditation techniques to other priests and the Catholic laity. They changed the word "mantra," which is used in Transcendental Meditation, to their new term "sacred word." The idea behind the "sacred word"— really, it's a "mantra"— is to use it as what I would call the "home button"; when you start to think of anything at all, you say that word and focus on it alone, and it brings you back "home." The goal is to totally empty one's mind, creating a mental void. Once you accomplish that, they say, you can achieve "pure consciousness" and find your "god-center," whatever that means.

In reality, this process can put you in a state of deep concentration. But it is not prayer. In fact, many believe that emptying one's mind that way can make a person susceptible to the diabolical, or evil spirits, which are all too real. The proponents of centering prayer claim that in using their technique, one can achieve true contemplative prayer. But Christian prayer is not done by emptying one's mind of everything; it is always being aware and focusing on the Holy Trinity, what Christ did for us, our thanks to Him, and our adoration of Him. True Christian prayer can never be devoid of what we believe and Who it is that offers us salvation. An excellent form of Christian meditation is the Holy Rosary.

Another term used in this technique is finding one's "true self." Evidently, when we are in our usual state of consciousness, we are our "false self." I find it fascinating that this devious concept was allowed to be introduced to the Catholic clergy and laity. To me, it goes to show the mindset that existed around the time of the Second Vatican Council: anything to change the present state of the Church is now acceptable and worthy of pursuit. It was a strange time indeed.

Thinking that true contemplative prayer can be achieved through the use of centering prayer is mystifying. When God grants one true contemplation, it's through true prayers of adoration, worship, and focus on who we are and Who it is that saves us. If one truly reaches that degree of faith, God may infuse you with the gift of contemplation. In seeking such a wonderful grace from God, emptying one's mind of every conceivable thought will not accomplish that.

Saint Teresa of Avila is often referred to by centering prayer proponents as one who performed that type of prayer, but that is disingenuous. Teresa often talked about genuine contemplative prayer. She is quoted as saying this:

"Taking it upon oneself to stop and suspend thought is what I mean should not be done; nor should we cease to work with the intellect, because otherwise we would be left like cold simpletons and be doing neither one thing nor the other. When the Lord suspends the intellect and causes it to stop, He Himself gives it that which holds its attention and makes it marvel and without reflection it understands more in the space of a Creed than we can understand with all our earthly diligence in many years. Trying to keep the soul's faculties busy and thinking you can make them be quiet is foolish."

There is a wonderful book written by Connie Rossini, titled, *Is Centering Prayer Catholic?* She is an excellent Catholic author who focuses on the subject of authentic contemplative prayer. Here is a quote from her educational book, which I suggest you read:

"What is the relationship between prayer and belief? The Catechism explains the old Catholic adage *lex orandi, lex credendi,* 'the law of prayer is the law of faith; the Church believes as she prays' (CCC no. 1124). Historically, Christian prayer came before the New Testament was written, before any Creed was formulated. Already before the first Pentecost, the disciples devoted themselves to 'the prayers' (Acts 1:14). Later, as the Church reflected on her prayers, she began to formulate the Creeds. In turn, greater insight into the divine mysteries and greater precision in Catholic doctrine led to a refining of the Liturgy. The Liturgy not only helps develop the Christian faith, it also expresses it (*CCC* no. 1126). Prayer and belief are intimately connected. When we err in one, the other suffers as well.

"This is true of personal as well as liturgical prayer. If a person practices a prayer method that is not in line with the ancient Catholic tradition, he may easily be led astray on basic beliefs that the Church defined long ago. So then, when we consider whether Centering Prayer is a legitimate part of the Christian tradition of prayer, we must consider the theology engendered by it. Most discussions of Centering Prayer fail to address theological questions adequately. In my own dialogs with Centering Prayer practitioners, I encounter many people who argue that their prayer method originated with the saints. But when I raise theological questions about Centering Prayer, the questions are largely ignored."[1]

Mindfulness

Another strange phenomenon brought about out of the New Age movement is termed "mindfulness." It also has its foundations in Buddhist meditation. Not only did many Catholics get caught up in this man-centered, contrived process, but companies around the world introduced it to their employees in an effort to get them to better focus on sales, presentations, business development, etc., selling it as another of the many self-improvement techniques that would enhance one's performance in a given area.

Involvement in mindfulness is an effort to get in touch with one's feelings, bodily sensations, and awareness of things as they are, whether bad or good, in an effort to acknowledge and accept them. Much like with centering prayer, one strives to enter an altered state of consciousness in order to achieve a sought-after result. It is said to bring about relaxation and relieve stress.

Everything about this method of self-improvement comes from Buddhist practices, such as "body scan meditation" and "breathing space meditation." The danger comes when Catholics attempt to include the concept of mindfulness in their spiritual practices. There is an important difference between this type of meditation and authentic Catholic meditation and prayer. While one is simply a self-centered mental exercise, the other is a way to adore and worship God.

Catholics who try to enhance their spiritual lives through the use of this method of meditation may be deluding or deceiving themselves and others, because this process can actually lead them away from God, which is not the intent, I'm sure. Performing these meditations are also supposed to help you accept who you are and what you do, right or wrong. That belies the truth that we are all sinners and should strive to correct our wrong and sinful actions. In short, Catholics should stay clear of the mindfulness process when praying or meditating. As Catholic Christians, we only need a strong faith in God, along with attending Mass and receiving the Holy Eucharist, and developing a consistent prayer life. When our total trust is in God, our worries, problems, and stress will be shouldered by Him. We can be absolutely sure of that.

In recent years, even schools are attempting to push mindfulness practices on students. Parents need to be vigilant when it comes to any new techniques that are meant to enhance students' performance in academics. Good, old-fashioned study habits and competent teachers is all they need. Unfortunately, the possible negative effects students and adults can experience as a result of using mindfulness meditations are of great concern. Some individuals have suffered from psychotic attacks, panic attacks, and feelings of being disconnected from others. Most people don't think twice about the bad things that can happen when delving into unknown areas regarding the mind. As Catholics, our compass, if you will, should be whether or not a particular practice is and has been given the thumbs-up by the Church. And by "the Church," I don't mean individual bishops and priests; I mean the Church as the teaching body of what Jesus Christ passed on to us. Let's face it, we have been misled many times by wayward clergy. Having said that, I must emphasize that I believe most priests are holy and of good intention. Knowing one's Catholic faith is the best protection against being led in the wrong or dangerous direction.

Chapter 4
More Catholic No-Nos

Countless people who are Catholic have decided that a great way to "exercise" is to join a yoga class. After all, it is a harmless act to add to other activities like walking, riding a bike, or lifting weights. They may have heard that it came from an ancient Hindu practice, but that's not what it is here in the United States. What possible harm can it do? I've heard those very sentiments from several Catholics.

Johnnette Benkovic, host of Women of Grace on EWTN, and an expert on all things New Age, wrote a book called *The New Age Counterfeit*, in which she states the following:

"Hatha yoga—salvation through physical exercises—physical manipulation of one's body to create an altered state of consciousness which occurs as a result of the effect of the exercise on the central nervous system.

"Japa yoga: the 'mechanical path to salvation'—the repetitious use of a mantra (sacred word), usually the name of a Hindu god or evil spirit. This creates a state whereby the mind is conscious but unaware of anything or any thought … called pure consciousness or transcendental consciousness."[1]

Remember centering prayer, during which one also uses a "sacred word"? Yoga and centering prayer are very close cousins. The long and short of it is that yoga is not acceptable for Catholics to be involved with. Stretching and relaxation can be done without using Eastern Hindu techniques, which are in every sense of the word "non-Christian." I urge all Catholics to stick to your Catholic roots and help restore your Catholic identity.

The Enneagram

A so-called simple personality test, called the Enneagram, came to prominence in the early 1970s. It was being promoted by a Jesuit priest, Father Bob Ochs. He began giving seminars on the subject to many, many young seminarians. One of the impressionable and curious seminarians at that time was Father Mitch Pacwa, S.J., a popular EWTN host and esteemed author. The symbol of the enneagram is a circle that is surrounding a nine-point star. The nine points purportedly represent separate personality traits. This author thinks it looks satanic. Maybe that's only me.

An Armenian occultist, George Ivanovich Gurdjieff, brought the enneagram to the West. It originated with Muslim mystics within the Sufi religion. While in Asia pursuing his study of the occult, he learned about the enneagram from these mystics. They utilized it for fortune-telling and a way to pursue "enlightenment." Sound familiar? These techniques and meditations are all interconnected.

"The Sufi and occult origins of the enneagram are generally unknown to many Christians because it is bathed in Christian-sounding language."[2]

Indeed, instruction on the use of the enneagram is included in many of the spiritual direction courses in the United States. Unsuspecting Catholics just follow the leader in these situations not realizing what they are being led into. It's another example of people just accepting things at face value and not questioning concepts that could be detrimental to their faith.

In a writing called "Enneagram Versus the Catholic Church," Rick Kephart opined:

"Catholics are using the Enneagram to talk about things like saints and sin and faith and 'fruits of the Spirit.' Using these words makes it sound legitimate. But they are only adapting these terms to the Enneagram, by giving them different definitions.

"For instance, 'sainthood' in the Enneagram has nothing to do with holiness. It has to do with the Sufi meaning of saint, which is a person who is illuminated to Reality. Therefore, in the language of the Enneagram, a saint is someone who 'overcomes his false self and knows and acts according to his true self.'"[3]

In the enneagram, the fruits of redemption have nothing to do with the salvation won for us by Christ; it means freeing oneself from his "false self" and becoming his "true self." It focuses on the all-important self. The devious leaders of this technique, as well as others we have discussed—whether they realize it or not—are leading unknowing Catholics into dangerous spiritual territory.

After being taken in with the enneagram and other non-Catholic fads, Father Mitch Pacwa, and other gullible priests, backed away from these things. Father Pacwa is, and has been for a long time, a wonderful teacher of the faith. In other words, those who sought the truth and studied these subjects from the heart of the Church were able to discover that truth. Others should follow that example. This quote comes from Father Pacwa:

"One gentleman heard one of my lectures on the ennea-gram and read my New Covenant magazine articles about it. When his parish was about to sponsor an enneagram workshop, he distributed the articles to parish council members so they could rethink the issue in light of more information. The seminars were not held.

"Sometimes nothing can be done about New Age events taking place in parishes and retreat houses. Sometimes a director of religious education, pastor, or other leader will not budge....

"This is not a call to be obnoxious, nor is it a summons to mobilize against everything we do not like. Our liking or disliking some incidental is not the issue at stake here. Rather, will we stand up for what is truly the Catholic faith, or will we allow false doctrine to be taught? When the issue is merely a matter of personal taste, we should learn to accommodate and compromise, learning to work with a variety of people within the church. But when someone contradicts clear Catholic doctrine, then we have an obligation, whether we are clergy or lay, to stand up for the church and its faith. The Nazis gained power in Germany when good people did little or nothing to stop them. The New Agers will dominate American Catholics unless those who see the errors stand up to the falsehoods."[4]

One would think that after all of the books, articles, and even Vatican documents warning against the use of the ennea-gram by Catholics, they would have taken them to heart and put this subject to rest. But, no, many directors of religious education, catechists, priests, nuns, and leaders of spiritual direction classes, persist in exposing unsuspecting Catholics to this misguided and faulty practice. Using the enneagram is not for Catholics in any way whatsoever, and when we see or hear that someone is teaching it, we must voice our objection to the powers that be. We must not and cannot remain silent in the face of actions that go against Church teaching. Using the enneagram is closely related to its cousins: tarot card reading, astrology, psychic predictions, and the like. Catholics beware.

Energy Healing

One of the biggest frauds ever perpetrated on mankind is the idea that everything and everybody share a source of energy, or a so-called "life force." As Catholics, we should be well aware that Jesus healed many people during His ministry on earth, and He also gave this ability to His Apostles. The source of that ability was Almighty God; in other words, it is a divine super-natural phenomenon.

Can energy be channeled from one person to another to produce a healing of the body or mind? Many claim that it can. This concept or idea also comes from the East, where most of these non-Christian "religions" reside. Various types of "energy healing" are very popular in the United States and around the world. No scientific proof exists that these techniques actually work; nonetheless, they are recognized and given credibility by, unbelievably, the National Institutes of Health in the United States of America. They must therefore be legitimate, right? No.

The use of energy healing techniques, such as Reiki, ther-apeutic touch, reflexology, etc., for all intents and purposes, is like using magic and sorcery. According to those who practice Reiki, one's pain or illness is because of an imbalance in one's "energy."

A good question to ask is: Where does the source of healing come from when performing this method? We Catholics have been warned by the Church that this type of procedure amounts to nothing but superstition. True healing comes from God alone. Many Catholics have been seduced by the devious purveyors of this untested, unscientific, and un-Christian snake oil healing method.

To give the reader an idea of how one becomes a practitioner of Reiki, consider this:

"Reiki is not taught in a traditional way in which a teacher instructs a student but is 'transferred' to the student by a Reiki master by means of an attunement. During the process, the Rei or God-Consciousness purportedly makes adjustments to the student's energy pathways to accommodate the ability to channel Reiki, then links the student to the Reiki source. The Reiki master does not direct the process but is simply a channel for the attunement energy flowing from the Higher Power."[5]

Chapter 5
"Gurus" Wayward Catholics Follow

Carl Gustav Jung was a psychoanalyst who was born in Switzerland in 1875. His mother was an occultist/spiritualist, while his father was a Lutheran minister. Even though it is apparently not well-know, Jung had a serious disdain for the Catholic Church, which became clear in his later work. That being the case, it is a mystery why many Catholics became very interested in and enamored by the theories Jung talked about and taught.

"It's certainly one of the most bizarre developments in 20th-century Catholicism that Carl Gustav Jung, dedicated to the destruction of the Catholic Church and the establishment of an anti-Church based on psychoanalysis, should have become the premier spiritual guide in the Church throughout the United States, Canada, and Europe over the last three decades.

"But that's the case.

"Walk into a typical Catholic bookstore and browse in the 'spirituality' section, and you'll see the best-selling books of such popularizers of the Jung Cult as priests Basil Pennington, Richard Rohr, and Thomas Keating."

Before continuing this particular quote, I'll just remind the reader that Fathers Thomas Keating and Basil Pennington were two of the developers of the centering prayer phenomenon we earlier discussed.

Continuing:

"Read the listings for 'spirituality' programs and retreats in many diocesan newspapers. You'll see that programs on Jungian dream analysis, discovering the child within, contacting your 'god/goddess,' or similar such Jungian therapy programs predominate, even though they have nothing to do with Catholic spirituality and are inherently antithetical to it.

"Forty years ago, the great Catholic psychiatrist Karl Stern (Harcourt Brace & Co., 1954) wrote that most Catholic scholars recognized that Jung and Catholicism are incompatible-irreconcilable, and he warned that the Jungian who begins viewing religion as existing on the same plane as psychology ends up viewing all religions as equally irrelevant."[1]

It is hard to believe that Catholics, both clergy and laity, have been taken in by an individual such as Carl Jung. By all accounts, when he was attending medical school, he developed a keen interest on the occult. It seems as though his mother was a bigger influence on him than his father. Instead of growing in Christianity, he went the opposite way. His attention turned to studying what a belief in God did to the psyche; he wanted to know what religion did to people and how their faith affected their lives. As for himself, he renounced Christianity in 1912.

Carl Jung and Sigmund Freud were contemporaries. They collaborated periodically, but they had a parting of ways over the idea that there is a sexual basis for neurosis. At one point in the early 1900s, Jung began having dreams and visions, eventually coming to believe that his house was haunted. He thought he saw ghosts. This experience moved him to write something he called "The Seven Sermons." He claimed to have had "spirit guides," to whom he gave the names "Philemon" and "Ka."

Eventually, Jung decided that in order to be a "whole" person, one needed to embrace his or her dark side as well as the good side. If that can be accomplished, one will have discovered the god within—or the true self. In other words, the "real" god is within us, or is us.

One consultant psychiatrist, Pravin Thevathasan, made this observation:

"Jung claimed to have identified three stages of religious evolution. The first stage was the archaic age of the Shamans. This was followed by the ancient civilisation of prophets and priests. Then came the Christian heritage of mystics. At every stage of religious history, all human beings share in the inner divinity, the numinous. When Jung talks about 'god,' he is really talking about the god within, the self. He was once asked if he believed in God. He answered: 'I don't believe. I know.' Thus, Jung made an act of faith in the existence of the collective unconscious and archetypes, and he interpreted Christianity in the light of his beliefs. As an example, let us examine the doctrine of the Trinity. For Jung, this doctrine is replete with psychological meaning. The Father symbolises the psyche in its original undifferentiated wholeness. The Son represents the human psyche, and the Holy Spirit the state of self-critical submission to a higher reality. For this myth to be authentic, it must be found in other cultures and Jung found similar Trinitarian ideas in the Babylonian, Egyptian and Greek mystical traditions.

"However, he believed in a Quaternity, the fourth person being the principle of evil. Without the opposition of satan, who is one of God's sons, the Trinity would have remained a unity. In Jungian terms, without the opposition of the shadow, or the fourth person, there would be no psychic development and no actualisation of the self. Jung came to believe that Mary became the fourth person following her Assumption. She is the necessary feminine element, the opposition of the shadow."[2]

To Carl Jung, a true and loving God is not a reality, but an idea, a nice thought for people needing a crutch. It was very interesting and amusing to him—and worth further study—that we weak-minded Catholics needed to cling to the beliefs that had been divinely revealed and passed down through the ages. Of course, he knew better, right? The fact that Catholic clergy introduced this ridiculous trash to unsuspecting laity is reprehensible, and it's even more astounding that the ideas and teachings of Carl Jung remain within the Catholic realm of thought and in our bookstores today.

Giving credence and credibility to people whose ideas and teachings are virtually opposite to those of the Church terribly erodes our identity and profanes the Body of Christ itself. Are there others that Catholics embrace which could hamper our road to salvation? You bet, and they are legion. Over the centuries, there have been many of these types of people roaming the earth seeking the ruin of souls, and we have many today.

Father Richard Rohr O.F.M.

Richard Rohr has been promoting error and heresy for many years in the Catholic Church. Unbelievably, he has been given free rein to do retreats around the country and to lead conferences on cruise ships—free for him, I'm sure. He is invited to speak at parishes and large Catholic conventions across the country. It's truly a mystery why any bishop would allow this, unless, of course, he agrees with his ideas and false teaching. Realizing that it's next to impossible to excommunicate or laicize a wayward priest these days, at the very least wouldn't it be appropriate—even expected—that bishops would be vocal in opposing the anti-Catholic words Rohr is spewing? This wayward, now-retired priest is a New Ager to his core and is a big proponent and promoter of the unscientific enneagram. He is a devoted follower of the aforementioned anti-Christian psychoanalyst Carl Jung, whose theories permeate everything Rohr does. This man poses a spiritual danger to Catholics; yet, we see his books in all of our stores.

It seems as though many Catholics have become interested in all things mystic, and Rohr has been referred to as being a modern-day mystic. Many of the retreats he has led have actually been diabolical in nature. I will describe what types of things occurred, but first it's necessary to explain his organization and tell you a little about the people he has working side by side with him.

Richard Rohr founded what is called the Center for Action and Contemplation (CAC). It has a teaching arm called the "Living School." If you want to move away from your Catholic identity and be led further from the truth, this is the place for you. The very first paragraph on the website's "Faculty" page says this: "The teachers at the Living School open Christianity up to a broader and more inclusive theological vision. They draw upon contemplative wisdom present in the Christian contemplative tradition, a lineage of individuals who experienced God as permeating all reality. Contemplative practices of self-emptying (kenosis) are the means by which we open ourselves to personally experience God's grace and to express God's radical compassion for suffering, particularly for the socially marginalized."

Exactly what is "contemplative wisdom"? And what do they mean by "God as permeating all reality"? Doesn't "self-emptying" sound a little like Transcendental Meditation and centering prayer? They have developed a language comprised of nice-sounding words that in actuality have no relationship to Christianity, especially Catholicism. In fact, I couldn't find the word "Catholic" on the website anywhere. Isn't Rohr a Catholic priest? Why is he so revered in Catholic circles around the United States?

Let's take a look at the faculty within CAC's Living School. I will not name these so-called teachers of Christianity, but I will enumerate their "credentials." One may visit the site if their identities are important for you to know.

First, they list a female described as a "modern-day mystic." She is an Episcopal priest and a retreat leader, among other listed accolades. It is her desire to "spread the recovery of the Christian contemplative and wisdom path." She has written several books, including one on centering prayer. Rest assured, she is not opposed to it. How would this person help to enhance our Catholic spirituality and aid us in retaining our Catholic identity?

Next is a clinical psychologist, who is also called a "contemplative teacher." He apparently does retreats for both men and women from all religious traditions. His short bio states that he was once a cloistered monk. He lived at the same Trappist monastery that—you guessed it—Thomas Merton inhabited. In fact, Merton was apparently his spiritual director while there. Didn't Merton study and promote Eastern mysticism and meditation? I thought so.

Then there is a Protestant Doctor of Philosophy, who claims to be a spiritual teacher who focuses especially on African-American spirituality, which I didn't realize was actually different than Asian, Hispanic, Caucasian, or any other ethnicity's Christian spirituality.

Last, they list a former Protestant pastor who advocates "a new kind of Christianity." He claims to also engage in "contemplative activism." Just what is that? According to him, he focuses on "caring for the planet, seeking justice for the poor, and working for peace." Who can be against those things, right? One of his books is titled *Why Did Jesus, Moses, the Buddha, and Mohammed Cross the Road.* I guess that about covers it all.

It will be fruitful for the reader to know a few tidbits about the retreats and conferences that Richard Rohr has taken part in over the years and why both faithful Catholics and Protestants should steer clear of anything offered by his organization.

Michael Hichborn of the Lepanto Institute published an article for LifeSiteNews back in 2018, which outlined some of the actions and untoward affiliations of Richard Rohr. Hichborn's investigations of entities that prove to be antithetical to the Catholic Church are very reliable and informative to clergy and laity alike. In this particular article he writes, in part:

"The CAC hosted a workshop inspired by Starhawk, a self-proclaimed witch and neo-pagan practitioner of goddess-worship....

"The CAC newsletter, The Mendicant, published a testimonial in 2014 with the following statement: 'I came to the

Living School simply because Richard Rohr had been the first, in my experience, to pray to 'Mother God' in a Mass.'

"The CAC promotes Labyrinth walking as well as the Enneagram.

"According to researcher Stephanie Block, Fr. Rohr told The New Ways Ministry Conference in 1997 that his all-male retreats (with both homosexual and heterosexual participants) often end with men spontaneously going nude and performing a healing ceremony 'laying hands' on each other.

"Fr. Rohr crudely states, 'We often have campfires, and I know some of you have been at these where it happens, so you know what I'm talking about. Always, always, there's some guys—I mean, is it in their hard wiring?—they'll strip and have to leap over that fire, burning their balls ... I don't know what it is. They're the 'real' men, who can leap over the fire, naked."[3]

Remaining truly Catholic means that we must resist anyone and anything that is attempting to draw us into the New Age "theology" and philosophies that exist. It is enough to simply adhere to our solid and constant Catholic Church teaching, which has endured from the beginning. Not everyone agrees with me, but I contend that the main reason for Catholics going astray and looking for something exciting and different is the simple fact that we don't know our faith well enough; if we did, these things wouldn't be so enticing to us and serve to influence our thinking, and we wouldn't look to other religions for guidance.

The blame for this problem rests squarely on the Church leaders, who decided over fifty years ago to water down and obscure the very important teachings that were handed down from the Church's earliest days.

Father James Martin, S.J.

There is another priest that has been loosed among the laity in the United States. He has chosen the mantle of being a great champion of the so-called LGBTQ community. He advocates for the idea that Catholics who oppose active homosexuality are just homophobes, nasty, and unloving people, who can't be true Christians. He contends that members of the same sex should be able to be blessed in marriage by the Catholic Church.

Martin writes books supporting his heretical ideas and, believe it or not, is invited to parishes all over the country to talk to and convince the laity that he is correct in his position. What does the fact that he is one of the most popular speakers in the Catholic world now tell us? In my opinion, when he is brought in to do his show, it tells me that the priest of that parish and the bishop of that diocese think what he promotes has merit.

Has active homosexuality always been a mortal sin, according to Scripture and Church teaching? Yes.

Has marriage always been defined as the divine union of a man and a woman, who can then possibly have children—in other words, a family? Yes.

Christians fully realize that one of the crosses a particular person may have to carry is a same-sex attraction, which is extremely unfortunate. We as Christians are called to help these people deal with their problem, not to help them commit sin. We all have crosses to bear of one type or another. The Christian way is to come to each other's assistance when we can. Simply feeling sorry for one who has a same-sex attraction doesn't mean that we should support them in that sin and imply that it's acceptable. True charity is to help them not sin in that way.

I realize that in today's topsy-turvy world, that is called being "politically incorrect" and "intolerant."

A somewhat disturbing fact is that Father Martin seems to be a close confidant of our current pope. It's very bothersome to me and others that he has had extensive private audiences with Pope Francis. It is my hope that the pope is scolding Martin and offering good spiritual direction. But is he?

There are several bishops in the United States and in other countries who openly support homosexuality and other offenses against Our Lord and His Holy Catholic Church, so Father James Martin is not on his own by any means. There is an active spiritual war going on not only in the world, but inside the Church itself. It is more important than ever before to study and learn the faith well, which in my case served to strengthen my relationship with God. I too remember being influenced by extraneous and erroneous diversions, until I had an experience that led to my eye-opening conversion. What happened to me is explained fully in my first book, *Christians Must Reunite: Now Is the Time.*

Chapter 6
Dissident Organizations

In addition to Richard Rohr's Center for Contemplative Action, Catholics—including priests, nuns, and laity—have associated themselves with several other organizations of questionable character and beliefs.

Presently, one of the most prominent Catholic-destroying groups calls itself the Association of U.S. Catholic Priests (AUSCP). It is an Ohio-based group that claims to be the largest priest organization of its kind in the United States.

Some of the AUSCP's major issues are astonishing to faithful Catholics. They advocate for women deacons (opening the door to women priests), who could run "priestless parishes"; the admission of known homosexuals into the priesthood, even though that has been strongly opposed in light of the recent sexual abuse scandals; weak immigration laws; strong climate change laws; strong opposition to the use of the death penalty, in spite of the fact that the Church has always supported it in egregious and rare circumstances. Their mission statement reads like a liberal-progressive political platform. When they state that former President Obama's Affordable Care Act should be upheld and enhanced so that health care premiums will be more affordable, they are oblivious to the fact that premiums have skyrocketed due to effects of that bill. Is this the type of

"ministry" a Catholic priest should be pursuing? This group of
over 1,200 priests acts more like a political action committee
than the holy men we desperately need to teach the faith and
lead souls to Christ. When they have as one of their objectives
and priorities that insurance companies "should be prevented
from discriminating against women," what exactly are they
referring to? The answer, in my opinion, is that they believe
abortion should be permitted and covered in insurance poli-
cies. What other segment of "women's health care" could they
be talking about? However, they stop short of admitting this,
letting it just hang there. Anybody who pays attention realizes
that when "women's health care" is brought up by progressives
in politics or in the Church, one can just substitute another
word: abortion.

Another dissident group that many Catholics have been
entangled with is the Center for Prophetic Imagination. What
could that possibly mean? Here are some of their "core principles," as listed on their website:

"1. Jesus Christ is our center and example for life.

"2. By encountering the living presence of God in prayer
and contemplation, we begin to experience the world propheti-
cally, as Jesus does.

"3. The prophetic imagination cannot be understood
apart from the lived experiences of marginalized and oppressed
people—including but not limited to those who are people of
color, queer, trans, femmes, gender nonconforming, Muslim,
formerly and currently incarcerated, cash poor and working
class, disabled, undocumented, and immigrant.

"4. Imperial structures and myths seek to alienate us from
one another, from the rest of creation, and from our Creator.

"5. Therefore, empowered by the Spirit, we will actively resist forces of alienation.

"6. As we encounter God in the midst of this struggle, we find new ways of human flourishing, for deep praxis deepens our prophetic imagination and shows us that a new world is possible.

"7. We become more like Jesus when we bring our full selves and deepening creative capacity into the task of co-creating the new world."

What is it they are saying? I have no clue, and I'm sure you don't either. Are they able to create prophets? Do we have to live as gays, transgenders, Muslims (I'm sure they would be happy to be included in this list), or illegal immigrants in order to develop a "prophetic imagination" and thereby become prophets ourselves? At this point, I'm tempted to say, "Well, sign me up," but since it might sound flippant, I won't do that. So I'm sorry that this Catholic won't be helping them "co-create a new world."

I will not mention all of the possible dissident groups that claim to be enlightened Catholics, because it would take many more pages to do so. However, I will point out one more that you may or may not be aware of. It's actually called Roman Catholic Women Priests (RCWP). Their claim to fame is that they are an international movement "within the Roman Catholic Church." You can read this on their website:

"The mission of Roman Catholic Women Priests is to prepare, ordain in Apostolic Succession, and support primarily women who are called by the Holy Spirit and their communities to a renewed priestly ministry rooted in justice and faithfulness to the Gospel.

"This international movement is operating worldwide with two groups formed in the USA referred to as Roman Catholic Womenpriests-USA (RCWP-USA) and the Association of Roman Catholic Women Priests (ARCWP). Both of these organizations have international members. These women priests are ministering in over 34 USA states and are also present in Canada, Europe, South and Central America, South Africa, Philippines and Taiwan."

This trendsetting bunch claims that they "ordain" qualified men and women "to serve the people of God as priests in a community of equals."

I've only touched the tip of the iceberg regarding the many purported Catholic organizations that seek to change the Church according to their own personal and "enlightened" ideas. When we as Catholics are taken in and enthralled by anyone or any group seeking to change the Church to keep up with the times, I suggest you run the other way. If we just stick with Christ and His immutable teachings that have been passed down through the ages, we can begin to recapture our Catholic identity.

Chapter 7

Where Have the Catholic Schools Gone?

There was a time when Catholic schools were very special institutions, where children could not only learn reading, writing, and arithmetic, etc., but they were also formed in the faith. The teachers were priests and nuns who helped develop the "whole" child, meaning general knowledge in the necessary academic disciplines, but they also molded their character and enhanced their belief in God to the extent they could. Having said that, the place where a child mainly learns his or her faith is in the family home. That was true then, and it's true now.

The problem is that it is difficult to pass on to your children that which you never learned yourself. That is the unfortunate conundrum we find ourselves in at this time. Over the years, owing to a huge reduction in priestly vocations and a precipitous drop in young women entering convents, Catholic schools have been forced to hire secular teachers in order to keep the schools viable. Obviously, these secular teachers had to earn more money than the priests and nuns did; otherwise, there was no incentive for teachers to even consider teaching at a Catholic school.

As a result of this development, Catholic schools had to raise the cost of tuition to cover their increased costs. The sad ensuing snowball effect was well on its way to ruining the

Catholic education process in the United States. The new secular teachers did not know the faith and, therefore, the Church's teachings were, for all intents and purposes, ignored. On top of all that, these teachers were not vetted regarding whether they were even Catholic, which has now yielded a devastating result. And even if some did identify as being Catholic, many of them were anything but that. It turns out that many among them were, and are now, part of the so-called LGBTQ community. We have seen incidents where parents have put pressure on the school administrations to correct the situation, so the teacher in question is fired, and the teacher then files a lawsuit against the school, which costs the school money to defend itself—and on and on and on.

What used to be called a "Catholic" school is more often termed a "private" school today. The cost to attend "private" schools is now prohibitive for many young Catholic families. They have become schools for the privileged children of high-income earning parents. The cost to attend some Catholic high schools rivals the cost of many universities.

Greg Dolan, Director of Policy and Outreach at Catholic Education Partners, wrote the following:

"A recent study in Education Next evaluates the shift in the haves and have-nots of private education, highlighting the disturbing trend of private schools enrolling students predominantly from high-income families. Authors Richard Murnane and Sean Reardon point to the loss of half of America's Catholic schools, and their mission to serve low-and-middle-income families, as a huge factor in this trend.

"While the authors point to two well-known causes of this decline, increased labor costs at Catholic schools and constraints on diocesan finances generally, the fact that as many people work for Catholic schools today as did in 1960, when there were twice as many schools and three times as many students, points to a serious lack of adaption on the part of Catholic school leaders.

"Murnane and Reardon state that 'private (elementary) schools, like public schools, are increasingly segregated by income,' with students from middle-income families half as likely to attend private school now compared to half a century ago. That downward trend comes as private schooling as a whole serves a smaller fraction of American schoolchildren— down from 15 percent in 1958 to less than 9 percent as of 2015.

"The authors argue that the decline in the number of Catholic schools, especially in urban areas, is a leading factor in the lack of affordable private schooling in the country. 'In 1965, 89 percent of American children who attended a private elementary school were enrolled in a Catholic school; in 2013, the comparable figure was 42 percent.' While Catholic schools were losing a huge share of students, average tuition rose from $873 in 1970 to $5,858 in 2010 (in 2015 dollars).

"What made Catholic schools increasingly price middle-income families out of a faith-filled education? The obvious explanation is a decline in religious vocations and the subsequent disappearance of low-cost labor from priests, nuns, and brothers on staff. But a fuller explanation shows that decades of Catholic school leaders did not adapt to changing circumstances to ensure that middle-income families would still be able to afford tuition.

"The National Catholic Educational Association reports that in 1960, 74 percent of school staff were members of religious orders or clergy; by 2017, religious staff represented less than 3 percent and lay staff now constitute nearly all staff in Catholic schools. Since lay people require a just and living wage, this creates a much more expensive model for Catholic schools. But leaders did not rethink the financial viability of their schools as the labor force completely changed around them. Instead, the numbers show Catholic schools replacing religious with lay staff at a one-for-one ratio over the past fifty years.

"From 1960 to 2017, half of Catholic schools closed (12,893 schools were cut to 6,429) and enrollment has been cut nearly by two-thirds (5,253,000 students vs. 1,878,824). Yet, during the same period, school staff has remained steady, with 151,902 staff in 1960 and 152,883 in 2017. As Catholic schools were shuttered, families left, and low-cost religious staff disappeared, Catholic school leaders kept staffing levels exactly the same."[1]

The bottom line in all this is that the salvific mission of the Church has been pushed aside in favor of buckling to a worldly, secular education that any child can really obtain in a public school. The only real difference is that a modern private school is inhabited by children with well-to-do parents. And Catholic they are not, in any way, shape, or form. The bottom line is that the almighty dollar and doing anything necessary to maintain the existence of "Catholic" schools have come at a tremendous cost: the loss of their authentic Catholic identity.

It seems as though most of our so-called Catholic universities have made a deal with the devil. They have given up on focusing on the faith and the Catholic intellectual tradition in favor of competing with secular universities in every respect. Many of those in the administrations of universities, such as the University of Notre Dame, Georgetown University, Catholic

University of America, and many others, have led these schools right off the cliff when it comes to their Catholic affiliation. The things they do that fly in the face of their original purpose are absolutely mind-boggling. And lest you think their school leaders have all been secular laypeople, think again. Most of them have been Catholic priests.

In the fall of 2016, a very prominent Catholic author and professor, Anthony Esolen, gave up his tenure at Providence College in Rhode Island in order to join the faculty at Thomas More College in New Hampshire. Why did he do that? Mr. Esolen could no longer remain at Providence because it had in essence lost its Catholicity. It seems that this particular professor believed that a classical Catholic education should be offered at a Catholic college instead of the so-called diversity courses that are now so popular. Providence was apparently walking away from its Catholic identity, even though they still like to refer to themselves as a Catholic college.

It's not unusual at all these days to see courses being offered at these mischaracterized schools, such as "gay and lesbian studies," "gender studies," and "social justice studies." Of course, the term "social justice" has a very different meaning in a secular context, which in many cases is actually anti-Catholic.

Many in the leadership ranks of several of our formerly Catholic universities decided somewhere along the way that it wasn't prudent to focus on the students' moral development at the same time as feeding their intellect. It's a mystery that Catholic priests would think this way; nonetheless, that's what they have done.

One of the priests that did grave damage to the University of Notre Dame was Father Theodore M. Hesburgh. In 1967, as president of that university, he, together with a group of other Jesuit priests, declared the university's independence from Catholic Church authority. That gathering of priests and others was in Land O' Lakes, Wisconsin. The decisions made at that conference got the ball rolling on many egregious offenses and acts of disobedience against the Church. Many priests and religious who made the decisions at these colleges were replaced with laypeople, and sacred statues and Crucifixes were removed from classrooms and campuses.

Theodore Hesburgh made it a habit to be disobedient to the Church, and he associated himself with many questionable causes and people. Case in point: He was a trustee and chairman of the board of the Rockefeller Foundation, which championed and funded abortion and population control efforts. Catholic? I think not.

In the 1960s, many priests in the Society of Jesus religious order (Jesuits) went off the rails and began to go their own way. It's important to say that not all of its members did so. There are a lot of holy and good Jesuit priests in the United States and around the world. However, many in their ranks began to flout the authority of the Church and resist many of its immutable teachings. Unfortunately, these Jesuits still wield a lot of power in the "Catholic" universities around our country. Catholics often think that if these priests believe some of the things they say and do on behalf of these schools, it must be in agreement with Church teaching. That is absolutely not the case.

The pursuit of money and the infiltration of liberal-progressive political administrators and professors have been allowed to infect Catholic higher education. Even as this has happened, outspoken alumni, students, and parents have opposed these travesties, but they have had very little success.

Since it was the Catholic Church that developed the university system, it is a shame that it has now been disregarded and pushed to the side. The first Catholic university was in Bologna, Italy, in 1088. In the United States, we are still blessed to have some solid Catholic colleges: Thomas More College in New Hampshire, Christendom College in Virginia, Ave Maria University in Florida, Franciscan University in Ohio, University of Dallas, and possibly a few others.

When there are so many working against the Catholic Church's presence at our universities, it makes it difficult to say the least. We as faithful Catholics need to make our voices heard and fight against the secularization of all of our great learning institutions. Sadly, the Catholic identity has been obliterated at most of our schools and universities. It is the secular belief that one cannot be formed in the faith and acquire worldly knowledge simultaneously. A lot of this mindset has to do with obtaining money from a largely anti-Christian government.

Chapter 8
Receiving Eucharist in the Hand

Since the Second Vatican Council, many changes have been made to the Liturgy. As mentioned earlier, the Novus Ordo Mass was supposedly devised in an effort to get the laity more engaged in the process. There are arguments made for and against this major change that include legitimate points.

As a Catholic who has studied Church history and learned the reasons for how and why certain things are done, I personally wish we had not changed the Mass. Having said that, I'm not one of those Catholics who believes that only the Traditional Latin Mass is legitimate. Yes, the Novus Order Mass is somewhat less reverent in various ways, but the main "ingredient" is still present: the consecration of the Holy Eucharist and the Precious Blood of Christ. Those attending both the Latin Mass and the Novus Ordo Mass receive the same body and blood of Jesus Christ.

Is receiving Our Lord on one's knees more reverent? Absolutely. Is receiving Our Lord on one's tongue more reverent? Positively. Of all the revisions in the New Mass, receiving communion on the hand while standing is the most egregious and offensive one. We still obtain the grace we need, provided we are in a state of grace when receiving, but in this author's opinion, we ought to revert back to the way we approached and received before Vatican II. The procedure we follow during communion time at Novus Ordo Masses has only fanned the flames of nonbelief in the Real Presence.

Are you aware that no pope has actually approved the act of receiving communion in the hand? That's a fact. However, at a time when bishops in Holland allowed it in an act of disobedience, the pope gave an indult, which allowed them to continue this erroneous practice. That was the opening needed for those who wanted this to be the norm. It was an unfortunate lapse of judgment by the pope.

As the abuse of communion in the hand increased and would soon begin in a few more countries, Pope Paul VI surveyed all bishops to see where they stood. The overwhelming majority of them rejected communion in the hand. As a result, the Congregation for Divine Worship concluded in a document called *Memoriale Domini,* "From the responses received, it is thus clear that by far the greater number of bishops feel that the present discipline (i.e., Holy Communion on the tongue) should not be changed at all; indeed if it were changed, this would be offensive to the sensibility and spiritual appreciation of these bishops and of most of the faithful."

Consequently, Germany, Belgium, and France followed suit and also began to offer communion in the hand. It is important to note here that not one of the sixteen documents that emanated from the Vatican II Council said anything about changing the way Catholics received the Eucharist. Nor did they advocate for allowing members of the laity to dispense communion. That came about, along with many other liturgical abuses, over the last 60 years. At first, laypeople who helped give communion were used very sparingly, and the name given to them was "extraordinary ministers." Now we hear them called "Eucharistic ministers." Actually, the only Eucharistic minister is the priest, and the lay ministers were originally supposed to be utilized in very extraordinary circumstances, in true cases of necessity, such as if the priest presiding is unable to do so for some reason. At the present time, churches have many, many extraordinary ministers, and the communicant is much more likely to receive from a layperson than from a priest at many parishes. It was never meant to be that way.

The act of receiving communion in one's hand did take place in the early Church, as some like to say in defense of this practice today. Saint Cyril warned against it in the fourth century, as did many others. It was probably originally instituted by the Arians, who denied the divinity of Christ. The Arian heresy was refuted by holy bishops and priests like Saint Athanasius of Alexandria. Regardless, communion in the hand continued until about the year AD 650, when it was condemned, and rightly so, but in several places the abuse continued. During the Synod of Rouen, in 878, this act was further decried. Since there were still some obstinate rebels in the Church that continued to distribute communion in the hand, it was determined then that greater reverence was due Our Lord in the host; that it should only be given by the consecrated hands of a priest. Another cogent reason was so that small particles of the Host would not be dropped or be left on the hands of the communicant. An added benefit—which is more likely to happen today—is that no one could make off with the Host in order to profane it in some way, or even use it in a so-called "black mass."

The "champion" of receiving the Eucharist in the hand in the United States was none other than Archbishop Joseph

Bernardin, one of the most egregious distorters of the faith within the Catholic Church in the United States. Unbelievably, he was president of what was then called the National Conference of Catholic Bishops (NCCB). Bernardin attempted several times to obtain the necessary two-thirds majority in favor of distributing communion in the hand, and he failed. Even after he left the top spot, he continued lobbying for his position. He worked to get the agreement of retired bishops and others that were absent for the votes. That was against the protocol for obtaining consensus, but that didn't concern him. After strong-arming some and calling in favors from others, he was able to garner the majority vote he needed to institute communion in the hand. This is only one of several nefarious acts performed by Bernardin to undermine Catholic teaching and seek to destroy our unique Catholic identity for years to come. The damage he has done to the faith is legend.

Saint Thomas Aquinas, in his extensive work on the faith, the *Summa Theologica*, gives us important insight into who should and should not touch, or dispense, the Eucharist. This section of the *Summa* answers objections regarding the minister of the Eucharist. Under the Third Article, the following objections and arguments are made:

"Whether Dispensing of This Sacrament Belongs to a Priest Alone"

We proceed thus to the Third Article:

"Objection 1. It seems that the dispensing of this sacrament does not belong to a priest alone. For Christ's blood belongs to this sacrament no less to His body. But Christ's blood is dispensed by deacons: hence, the blessed Lawrence said to the blessed Sixtus (Office of S. Lawrence, Resp. at Matins):

'Try whether you have chosen a fit minister, to who you have entrusted the dispensing of the Lord's blood.' Therefore, with equal reason the dispensing of Christ's body does not belong to priests only.

"Objection 2. Further, priests are the appointed ministers of the sacraments. But this sacrament is completed in the consecration of the matter, and not in the use, to which the dispensing belongs. Therefore, it seems that it does not belong to a priest to dispense the Lord's body.

"Objection 3. Further, Dionysius says (Eccl. Hier. iii, iv) that this sacrament, like chrism, has the power of perfecting. But it belongs, not to priests, but to bishops, to sign with the chrism. Therefore, likewise, to dispense this sacrament belongs to the bishop and not to the priest.

"On the contrary, It is written (De Consecr., dist. 12): 'It has come to our knowledge that some priests deliver the Lord's body to a layman or to a woman to carry it to the sick: The synod therefore forbids such presumption to continue; and let the priest himself communicate the sick.'

"I answer that, the dispensing of Christ's body belongs to the priest for three reasons. First, because, as was said above (Article 1), he consecrates as in the person of Christ. But as Christ consecrated His body at the supper, so also He gave it to others to be partaken of by them. Accordingly, as the consecration of Christ's body belongs to the priest, so likewise does the dispensing belong to him. Secondly, because the priest is the appointed intermediary between God and the people; hence, as it belongs to him to offer the people's gifts to God, so it belongs to him to deliver consecrated gifts to the people. Thirdly, because out of reverence towards this sacrament, nothing touches it, but what is consecrated; hence, the corporal and the chalice are consecrated, and likewise the priest's hands, for touching this sacrament. Hence, it is not lawful for anyone else to touch it except from necessity, for instance, if it were to fall upon the ground, or else in some other case of urgency.

"Reply to Objection 1. The deacon, as being nigh to the priestly order, has a certain share in the latter's duties, so that he may dispense the blood; but not the body, except in case of necessity, at the bidding of a bishop or of a priest. First of all because Christ's blood is contained in a vessel, hence there is no need for it to be touched by the dispenser, as Christ's body is touched. Secondly, because the blood denotes the redemption derived by the people from Christ; hence, it is that water is mixed with the blood, which water denotes the people. And because deacons are between priest and people, the dispensing of the blood is in the competency of deacons, rather than the dispensing of the body.

"Reply to Objection 2. For the reason given above, it belongs to the same person to dispense and to consecrate this sacrament.

"Reply to Objection 3. As the deacon, in a measure, shares in the priest's power of enlightening (Eccl. Hier., v), inasmuch as he dispenses the blood; so the priest shares in the perfective dispensing (ibid.) of the bishop, inasmuch as he dispenses this sacrament whereby man is perfected in himself by union with Christ. But other perfections whereby a man is perfected in relation to others, are reserved to the bishop."[1]

It's somewhat disingenuous for bishops and priests to refer to Saint Thomas Aquinas as a great Catholic philosopher and Doctor of the Church—which he absolutely was—and then

totally ignore or disagree with some of his most important conclusions regarding the Eucharist. I can only assume, based on
the fact that most people in the Novus Ordo churches receive
communion in the hand, that contemporary priests and bishops
believe it is the preferred way of doing so. Actually, it was always
meant to be the exception. Also, when children are preparing
for their first communion, most are only taught to receive in the
hand; however, to be fair, that is not always the case.

I and other defenders of receiving Eucharist on the tongue
contend that it is the most sanitary way to do it. Presumably,
the priest's hands are clean—or they should be—before distribution. Since one really should be kneeling to receive Our Lord,
like it once was, it is a better angle from which to dispense the
Host. When a paten is held under the communicant's chin while
receiving, fragments of the Host will not be dropped. I've personally seen one of the terrible things that can happen, which is
that a person can walk away with the Host in his or her hand. As
I related in my book *Christians Must Reunite: Now Is the Time*,
I witnessed an individual grab the Host with his thumb and
forefinger, say, "Thank you," and walk away with it. After Mass,
I confronted the priest about letting that happen. His response
to me was, "Well, hopefully, it will end up in the right place." I
have no idea what he meant. But I don't think that he believes in
the Real Presence; otherwise, he would not have let that happen.
In fact, one time I witnessed a holy priest chase down a woman
who walked away and didn't consume the Host. To him, it was
so important that he held up the others in line to retrieve Our
Lord. That particular incident happened at my son's wedding,
during which the priest carefully explained that only Catholics
in a state of grace should approach for communion; others could

approach with their arms crossed over their chests to receive a blessing if they desired. I guess some people just don't listen.

The so-called "reformers" in the early 16th century began distributing communion in the hand as a way of exhibiting their unbelief in the Real Presence of Jesus Christ in the Eucharist. They obviously didn't want their new followers to have any question about where they stood. The disappointing thing about that is that it must have put doubts in the minds of many bishops and priests, which has infected the Church ever since.

One of the most well-respected bishops in the modern world is Bishop Athanasius Schneider of Kazakhstan, in central Asia. He is a major proponent of receiving communion on the tongue while kneeling. The bishop wrote a short, but very important book on the Eucharist. I highly recommend reading this important work.

Bishop Schneider concluded his book with this statement, which I think would be fruitful for all bishops, priests, and the laity:

"God willing, the pastors of the Church will be able to renew the house of God which is the Church, placing the Eucharistic Jesus in the center, giving Him the first place, making it so that He receive gestures of honor and adoration also at the moment of Holy Communion. The Church must be reformed, starting from the Eucharist! *Ecclesia ab Eucharistia emendanda est!* The Church must be reformed by the Eucharist.

"The sacred host is not some *thing*, but some *One*. 'He is there,' was the way St. John Mary Vianney synthesized the Eucharistic Mystery. Therefore, we are involved with nothing other than, and no one less great than, the Lord Himself:[2] *Dominus est!* (It is the Lord!)."[3]

It would be very wise for the Church around the world to bring back to all dioceses and parishes the reverence due Our Lord Jesus Christ. That would entail returning all tabernacles to where they should be, elevated on the altars. We need to make Christ the center of it all. Catholic churches were never meant to be concert halls or venues for all of the different activities that now take place in them. And while we do that, Catholics need to be re-taught that contained in that little Host we all approach so irreverently these days is actually Christ's body, blood, soul and divinity. The recent Pew Research study, which concluded that about 70 percent of Catholics believe that the Eucharist is just a symbol, should drive that point home.

If Jesus appeared in front of you right now, would you kneel in His presence? I would hope so! Why did we ever take out communion rails and stop kneeling to receive Him in church? It's no different. As Catholics, our faith compels us to believe in certain things. If we truly believed, and knew ahead of time, that we would be approaching Our Lord, would we wear flip-flops, short-shorts, and cut-off shirts? Not on your life.

Where is the reverence?

Where is the belief?

Where are the holy bishops that will stop this crisis of the faith?

Where are the brave pastors who will defend the orthodoxy of the faith and make the necessary changes in their parishes, while promoting the truth?

To be fair and charitable, I know of several good and faithful bishops and priests who are doing their very best to accomplish these things. Sadly, they are in the minority, as most of them just go along to get along. It takes a special and brave member of the clergy to run against the wind, and I realize that. But, in all honesty, God and His Beloved Son deserve no less. Let's return to worshipping God as we should. Let's restore our Catholic identity!

Chapter 9
New "Catholic" Programs

Probably as a result of the mass exodus from the Catholic Church and the lack of young men entering seminaries to become priests—especially heterosexual ones—a trend started whereby new programs were being developed to garner the interest and approval of parishioners. Instead of devising and promoting programs that would teach Catholics more about their faith and serve to increase their faith, many of them were, and are, severely watered-down feel-good types of gatherings that are nothing more than social events.

Some of the very people bringing these weak programs to parishes are none other than the ones tasked with teaching the faith—the directors of religious education, many of whom have a woeful knowledge of Church teachings themselves. Again, I'm not lumping all directors of religious education (DRE) together; there are some I am aware of that are well formed and excellent teachers, possessing the requisite knowledge to impart accurate Catholic teaching to both children and adults.

Having put some blame on DREs, I must say that the true decider of what is presented to laity at a parish is the church's pastor. Going further, the purpose and mission of the bishops of dioceses is to teach the true faith. The bishops all need to be aware of what teachings are being offered at all of the parishes under his tutelage. If he does not do this, he is derelict in his duty.

One of the good programs that has stood the test of time is the Cursillo Movement, which is a weekend retreat that men and women do separately. It focuses on making better Christians of the attendees. While one "lives" a Cursillo, he or she will participate in adoration, rosary, way of the cross, daily Mass and will hear talks on the sacraments, piety, study and action. Having experienced Cursillo myself, I can honestly say it was an experience that served to strengthen my faith.

There are several very weak, non-Catholic programs that have come down the pike that are actually detrimental to parishioners. I am going to focus on the one I believe to be the most popular. It is called Alpha for Catholics, and its twin brother is ChristLife; they are one and the same. When I henceforth refer to Alpha, I will be talking about both.

Alpha is a Protestant concoction. It was first developed at a London Anglican parish. Its foundation comes from Charismatic Protestantism. The director and main promoter of the program has been Rev. Nicky Gumbel—not a Catholic, of course.

Pastors at Catholic parishes have been sold a faulty bill of goods in the hopes of forming better Christians, who will get more involved in the parish and probably support it more financially. The lay leaders who actually administer the program are "trained" in what to do and how to do it. They are explicitly taught not to "teach," but to focus on feelings and a personal relationship with Jesus Christ. Never mind that Catholics are very intimate with Christ because of our faith, but mainly because of the Eucharist. If an attendee begins to talk about the sacraments, the leaders are taught to redirect the subject matter to simply loving Jesus and reading the Bible.

When one arrives for the first of sixteen sessions of Alpha, dinner is served to all. Depending on the number of attendees, the people are divided up at several tables, with two lay leaders at each table. Following dinner, the whole group is shown a video. The idea is to talk about what they just saw, while the leaders ask scripted questions, which directs and drives the ensuing discussion.

Unbelievably, they avoid any discussion on the saints, and especially Our Blessed Mother Mary. The program seems to be more suited to non-believers, but of course the overwhelming majority of those attending are baptized Catholics. It starts out by letting everyone know that they need a personal relationship with Jesus; so far so good. They teach that if you just believe in Jesus, you're a Christian. But we know as Catholics that even Satan believes in Jesus, so faith alone is not enough. *Sola fide*, or "faith alone" is a mistaken Protestant concept.

Alpha teaches that Jesus took away all guilt and shame forever from us when He died for our sins. In truth, the Church teaches that we need to feel shame when we sin, and the way we return to a state of grace is to go to reconciliation. Talking about confession to a priest is a big no-no to the developers of this unfortunate program. According to them, the primary way God communicates with us is through the Bible, when in reality the Bible states that the *Church* is the "pillar and foundation of the truth" (1 Timothy 3:15). That means, of course, that Church Tradition (teaching by word of mouth passed down from the Apostles) has equal weight when it comes to passing on the faith.

As we should know as Catholics, the interpretation of Scripture is subject to the Church's teaching through its Magisterium. Interpreting Scripture oneself can lead to deciding one's own morality. We human beings tend to interpret things in ways that benefit us personally. The Church's teaching has never changed, and it will never change; it has remained constant from the beginning.

Believe it or not, the Anglican Church rejected the Alpha program in the beginning because they found it problematic from a Christian perspective. Eventually, it was accepted unchanged. It found its way into the Catholic Church—again unchanged—and is utilized in hundreds, maybe thousands, of parishes in the United States. The sellers and promoters of Alpha claim that it is just a launching pad to Christianity. The fact that it has been bought and paid for by many Catholic dioceses and parishes is a real mystery, since Catholics are already Christians. The promoters and sellers of this non-Catholic program are making a lot of money, while misleading bishops and parish pastors into thinking it will make people better Catholics and add to their bottom line. That is shameful, to say the least.

As a Consecrated Marian Catechist, back in 2015, I received an urgent email from our apostolate's international director and mentor, Raymond Leo Cardinal Burke. This was addressed to all Marian Catechists across the world:

"It has come to my attention that a program called 'Alpha in a Catholic Context' has been recommended to some Marian Catechists. Having studied the program, both from the perspective of doctrine and methodology, I must make it clear that the program may not be used, in any form, in the Marian Catechist Apostolate and that Marian Catechists are not to become involved with it. While like so many similar programs, Alpha may seem to offer a more attractive and effective form of evangelization and catechesis, it does not have the doctrinal and methodological foundations required for the teaching of the Catholic faith. Marian Catechists should continue to use the *Catechism of the Catholic Church,* together with the courses of the Servant of God Father John A. Hardon, S.J., and my *Commentary on the General Directory for Catechists.* I recall to all Marian Catechists the words of Pope Saint John Paul II in his Apostolic Letter *Novo Millenio Ineunte,* regarding those who think that, before the challenge of a new evangelization, the Church needs to discover 'some magic formula' or invent a 'new program': 'No, we shall not be saved by a formula but by a Person, and the assurance which he gives us: "I am with you."'

"The saintly Pontiff reminded us that the program by which we are to address effectively the great spiritual challenges of our time is, in the end, Jesus Christ alive for us in the Church. He explained: 'The program already exists; it is the plan found in the Gospel and in the living Tradition, it is the same as ever. Ultimately, it has its center in Christ Himself, who is to be known, loved and imitated, so that in Him we may live the life of the Trinity, and with Him transform history until its fulfillment in the heavenly Jerusalem. This is a program which does not change with shifts of times and cultures, even though it takes account of time and culture for the sake of true dialogue and effective communication' (no. 29).

"The Servant of God Father John A. Hardon, S.J., understood profoundly the truth of Pope John Paul II's words and, through the spiritual and doctrinal formation of the Marian Catechist Apostolate, as he so faithfully and wisely developed it,

Marian Catechists understand the same truth and are not allured or deceived by stories of a 'magic formula' or a 'new program.' In short, Marian Catechists understand that our program is holiness in life, which flows from a profound knowledge and ardent love of Christ, Who is alive for us in the Church."

To further bolster the points I am making against the Alpha program, I will refer to a 1999 article by Gillian Van der Lande, who did an exhaustive study on the subject. After discussing Alpha sources, ecclesiology, methodology, sacramental theology, and other important aspects to consider, the author's basic conclusion is that Alpha is very weak and flawed and should not be considered a preparation course for those entering RCIA. For the most part, though, it's being offered to long-time Catholics, which doesn't even make sense. Ms. Van der Lande concludes her piece by adding this quote by Rod Pead, Catholic editor of Christian Order Magazine (UK):

"The latest in the long line of New Age/Protestant Trojan horses to be wheeled into Catholic parishes with episcopal blessing is ALPHA. Zealous in its application of commercial principles to feel-good evangelization, ALPHA is big business— built on copyrights, target figures, line charts and multi-million-pound advertising campaigns. It emerged from Holy Trinity Brompton (HTB), an Anglican church behind the Brompton Oratory in London. In recent years, this church has ventured to the furthest edge of the Charismatic movement in its promotion of the Toronto Blessing—a so-called Baptism of the Holy Spirit which induces hysterical, animal-like behavior (uncontrolled laughter, shaking, gibberish, grunting, howling, etc.) among congregations. Mr. Nicky Gumbel, who introduced this alien 'spirit' into England via HTB in 1994, is the prime mover behind

ALPHA: 'I believe it is no coincidence,' he stated in May 1995, 'that the present movement of the Holy Spirit (Toronto Blessing) has come at the same time as the explosion of the ALPHA Course; I think the two go together.'

"One would have thought this connection alone sufficient to alert Catholic bishops and priests to keep their distance from ALPHA; to dissuade them from flirting with 'angels of light' (2 Cor. 11:13-15). Alas, such is their general loss of faith and blind panic at the massive yearly decline in the Catholic population that our Shepherds have rolled out the red carpet instead. Bishop Ambrose Griffiths of Hexham and Newcastle, who says that church attendance in his diocese 'has been going down on a straight line graph for the last 25 years,' has embraced ALPHA with uncanny zeal. Cardinal Hume, too, gave his blessing and personal message of encouragement to the 450 priests and laity who attended an ALPHA instruction course at Westminster Cathedral Hall in May 1997, conducted by Sandy Millar and Nicky Gumbel of HTB. The Cardinal claims to know people who have been helped by ALPHA—apparently oblivious to the many 'apparitions' and programmes like RENEW that promote serious error but claim 'conversions.'

"'I am sure it will be of great benefit to the Church's mission,' Bishop David Konstant has prophesied of ALPHA. 'It doesn't contain anything that is contrary to Catholic doctrine,' states Bishop Griffiths. After reading Mrs. Van der Lande's Objective analysis of an ALPHA course in a Catholic parish, readers may consider 'hirelings' too complimentary a label for such Shepherds."[1]

Bishops and pastors who allow Alpha to be purchased and presented to Catholic laity apparently don't realize the program does nothing to make the true Church the desirable choice, because what it does is put all Christian denominations in the same category. Really, for the Catholics who think our Church has "too many rules," it may—and probably does—send them to the feel-good, anything-goes Protestant church across the street. Is that what is meant by the "new evangelization"? I think not. While we love our Protestant brothers and sisters in Christ, our mission is to gently bring them back to the Church Jesus Christ founded: the Holy Catholic Church. Like Cardinal Burke and Pope Saint John Paul II both said, we already have the "program." Instead of it being "basic Christianity," as it is presented and sold to parishes, Alpha is nothing but "Charismatic Protestantism."

This Alpha program is the last thing we need in a Catholic Church that has been losing its identity for several decades. The Church is in a state of mass confusion on many levels. The average Catholic doesn't know what to believe anymore. Why do you think it is that Catholics feel it is appropriate to support politicians who vote for legislation that is in direct opposition to Catholic teaching? It is because most of those in the laity don't believe the Church teaches that way anymore, even though the teachings have never changed. I've heard people say things like: "I know she votes for abortion rights, which I don't believe in, but I like everything else she supports, like same-sex marriage and transgender rights; they are human beings, too." This can only be due to the lack of catechesis or a blatant nonbelief in Church teaching. These people may as well go join a Protestant denomination, because they aren't Catholic anyway.

No, I'm not suggesting that Catholics who don't know the faith go ahead and join a non-Catholic church. What I am suggesting is that our bishops and pastors start to promote actual Catholic teaching. Why can't they offer dinner and then show videos to parishioners that expand on the specifics of Catholicism? Following that, they can have question and answer sessions. It would be great! Why can't they bring in speakers that will help make it more exciting to be Catholic again. I truly believe that if they focus on restoring our Catholic identity, people will be invigorated in the faith. It could have the effect of incentivizing Catholics to entice non-Catholics to "come back home." As it is now, due to the mistakes and missteps of the last half century, we are only one of the tens of thousands of Christian choices. To minimize Christ's Church is a huge mistake.

Chapter 10
Where Have the Beautiful Churches Gone?

In previous chapters, we talked about some of the people who have led us away from our Catholic Church and attempted to change our identity. Also, we've discussed the types of programs being introduced into our parishes that serve to confuse us, including many that lead Catholics to leave the Church. There is another very important aspect of the unfortunate metamorphosis the Church has experienced that bears mentioning.

Many decades ago, when one entered a Catholic church, there was no mistake that it was indeed God's house. First of all, the outside of the building was beautiful and ornate, with big welcoming doors. The palatial structure was probably stone or brick, and the windows were large with stained glass. Usually, there was a bell tower from which that wonderful sound emanated, beckoning the parishioners and letting them know that the Holy Mass was about to begin.

Upon entering the narthex, the sense of holiness was apparent. Often, at one end would be the baptistery. At the several entry points into the nave would be a stoup containing holy water, making it easy for each person entering to bless themselves, bringing to mind their baptism. When parishioners entered the nave, it was understood that, for all intents and purposes, you were on holy ground. Silence and reverence were expected, for that is when the worship of Our Lord began. When entering your chosen pew, you would genuflect and make the sign of the Cross. While kneeling, you would say your initial prayers and ready your mind and heart to receive Christ in the Eucharist at the appropriate time.

As you sat quietly looking around before the commencement of the sacred Liturgy, you would observe the Stations of the Cross, sacred art, and statues of Our Lady and the saints. The reredos (wall behind the altar) would have niches for statues and possibly be painted with a biblical scene of some type.

Right behind the precious stone-made altar would be what was always meant to be the center of it all, the reason for being there: Christ's body, blood, soul and divinity in a beautiful gold tabernacle for all to behold and adore. We should do no less for the King of Kings, our Creator, right? But the winds of change were blowing in and infecting many in the Church with the plagues of secularism and modernism. Catholic churches were about to be made nothing more than nondescript, plain, white-washed buildings that could be used for any old secular purpose. Our Lord's tabernacles were banished to backrooms, called "reservation chapels." With Christ out of the way, the nave could be utilized in several different ways, limited only by one's imagination. Based on the myriad of abuses that came after Vatican II, some might believe that is when the modern church architecture began, but that's not the case; although, it certainly picked up steam after that Council.

Father Hans Ansgar Reinhold was a Catholic priest from Germany, who took refuge from the Nazis in the United States after World War II. In the late 1940s, he began his quest to reform Catholic church architecture so that it would be, in his opinion, "more functional." He wrote a book called *Speaking of Liturgical Architecture* in 1952. Father Reinhold also had a hand in the changes in the Liturgy that came about after Vatican II, which is not surprising. His modernistic ideas became widely accepted and adopted by Catholic laity and clergy, and architects especially liked the challenge of being artistic and innovative in redesigning Catholic churches. The race was on, but the damage these changes brought about was devastating to the Church's image and identity, and we are still living with the unsightly and unworthy Church buildings that exist in many parishes today.

Michael S. Rose, who was trained in architecture and the fine arts, has written a very important book, aptly entitled, *Ugly As Sin: Why They Changed Our Churches from Sacred Places to Meeting Spaces—and How We Can Change Them Back Again.* He points out on the back of his book, "The problem with new-style churches isn't just that they're ugly—they actually distort the Faith and lead Catholics away from Catholicism."

On a personal note, my wife and I were once in Richmond, Virginia, for the weekend. Before leaving in the late afternoon to return home to Williamsburg, after doing an internet search we found a local Catholic church where we could attend Mass. Upon entering the parking lot, my wife remarked, "That doesn't look like a church, but that's what the sign says." I agreed. We followed other people through the one set of glass double doors into what resembled a school building. The narthex was devoid of anything Catholic looking, but had a few tables with pamphlets on top.

Again, following the people, we went through another glass double door, where people were bottlenecked and waiting to bless themselves in the one large receptacle containing holy water—presumably also the baptistery. The interior of the church was a half circle, with the altar "down" on the floor in the center. I say "down" because the seating resembled a high school gym, and we had to climb up steps to sit in a pew with no kneelers. We said our prayers in preparation of the Mass. As we looked around, my wife said to me, "Are you sure this is a Catholic church?" All I could say was, "I know." The focal point from our perspective was the "band's" instruments, including drums, electric bass guitar, acoustic guitars, tambourines, and microphones.

Nowhere in sight was a Crucifix, or sacred statues, or paintings of saints, or Stations of the Cross. When the priest processed in with his female altar servers, we spotted the only Crucifix as one of the girls carried it. During Mass, the priest seemed to wing it with some of the liturgical language, using his own nice-sounding words. To say the least, my wife and I felt like we were at a Protestant service—except that we were able to receive the Eucharist, thankfully.

When Mass was ended, as we began to exit, I decided to approach the deacon (the priest was talking to several people).

I said hello and asked him, "Where is everything Catholic?"

He asked, "What do you mean?"

I then said, "I don't see the tabernacle, the Stations of the Cross, paintings or statues of the saints, and the music was Protestant-sounding folk songs." I give him credit for not getting mad at me, which was charitable in light of the question I just asked him.

He pointed to a hallway and said, "If you walk down the hall and enter the second door on the left, you'll find the tabernacle.

And over there is another hallway that contains the Stations of the Cross on the walls. The music we have here is what the congregation prefers because it's faster and more uplifting than what you hear at many Catholic churches. We kind of do our own thing." I thanked him for his help and we left.

Michael S. Rose points out in his excellent book:

"One basic tenet that architects have accepted for millennia is that the built environment has the capacity to affect the human person deeply—the way he acts, the way he feels, and the way he *is*. Church architects of past and present understood that the atmosphere created by the church building affects not only how we worship, but also what we believe. Ultimately, what we believe affects how we live our lives. It's difficult to separate theology and ecclesiology from the environments for worship, whether it's a traditional church or a modern church. If a Catholic church building doesn't reflect Catholic theology and ecclesiology, if the building undermines or dismisses the natural laws of church architecture, the worshiper risks accepting a Faith that is foreign to Catholicism."[1]

Not only do we in the United States seem to have lost our sense of history when it comes to the progress and the mistakes we have made as a nation, many in the leadership of the Catholic Church are forgetting the Church's beautiful and rich history. Catholic church buildings used to be built to last for generations. Instead of ornate, strongly built structures displaying all things Catholic, now they are cheaply built, plain-looking structures that probably won't last fifty years. If the building's sign is removed from one of these modern Catholic churches, they could easily make it a Protestant church the next day, or they could turn it into a gym facility, or they could make some of them concert venues; they could even install a bar in the "narthex." But I digress.

"Architects of future generations need to comprehend the language of church architecture in order to build permanent sacred edifices for their own times and future centuries. No successful church architecture can be—or even pretend to be—ignorant of the Church's historical patrimony. Continuity demands that a successful church design can't spring from the whims of man or the fashion of the day. The architect who breaks completely with architectural tradition robs his church of the quality of permanence that is essential to any successful church design. An authentic Catholic church building is a work of art that acknowledges the previous greatness of the Church's architectural patrimony: it refers to the past, serves the present, and informs the future."[2]

The bell towers in beautiful cathedrals and even smaller churches have been a real sight to behold and a beautiful sound to listen to over hundreds of years, and everyone just knew they were Catholic. Those days are all but gone. During a trip to Ireland several years ago, as we went by some gorgeous, old churches, the tour guide said several times, "That was formerly a Catholic church, but now it's Lutheran (or some other church)." Unfortunately, the country of Saint Patrick seems to be losing its Catholicity. I personally love hearing the bells toll at my own parish church before Mass; it's that call that tells us to come and worship the King of Kings.

"Not only does the church serve as a beacon by its situation on the heights or its rising high above the cornfields, but it's audible, too. Through its bells, the pilgrim is reminded of Christ's presence, His importance in the lives of the faithful, and our need to honor Him in adoration and prayer. All tolls and peals of the church bells, no matter what the occasion or time of day, are a summons to prayer—whether for the souls of the faithful departed, for the pious recitation of the *Angelus*, or as a call to worship through participation in the Holy Sacrifice of the Mass.

"The pilgrim can't help but be profoundly moved by the peal of cathedral bells, by the ebullient ringing of wedding bells, or by the mournful toll of the funeral bell. For our pilgrim, that distant sound may well be the first indication that his destination isn't far off. He then looks forward to catching his first glimpse of the church tower or spire rising above the urban fabric or seeing the silhouette of the church building atop a distant hill.

"The bell tower, often called the *campanile,* is one of the primary elements that draws the pilgrim to the church from a great distance, not only by the sound of its bells, but by its visual profile. Pointing upward to the heavens, it's a welcoming sign to pilgrims and tourists, parishioners and merchants alike."[3]

I hope and pray that the bishops and priests of the Catholic Church begin to institute some changes that will make our churches fit for Our Lord again. They are the ones who can make it happen, and we in the laity can help by asking them to do it— indeed insisting that we need to restore our Catholic identity by making our churches Catholic once again.

Chapter 11

Will You Be "Left Behind"?

Back in the late 1990s, a friend recommended a book that was all the rage among Christians. He told me it was fiction with regard to the characters, but that it was based on Scripture and an event that was destined to happen one day. That cataclysmic world event would be what they called the "secret rapture."

This so-called "true" event—the rapture—would happen before the end of the world. The book, *Left Behind*, enthralled and captured the attention of Christians—so much so that it became a very popular series of books. It seemed that both Catholics and Protestants bought into what the books portrayed as something that was inevitable in the history of humanity.

When I began reading these books, I was like most Catholics were at the time (and many still are); I was ignorant about my Catholic religion because I was never taught it properly. And like most, I didn't read Scripture enough and make it my business to study and learn it. I highly recommend that new and veteran Catholics start studying their faith more completely so that we don't just buy all the error being peddled in the world. A good start would be to obtain a copy of my first book, *Christians Must Reunite: Now Is the Time*. It will give you a solid foundation upon which to build. I was easily fooled into thinking that the so-called rapture would really happen someday. At that time, I had temporarily left the Catholic Church and was attending a Baptist church. I tell this story in my first book and, as you know, I returned to the true Church once I started learning what the actual teachings were.

I highly recommend a book that was written by Paul Thigpen, Ph.D., a former evangelical Protestant turned Catholic. He has written many excellent books from which you can glean much about your faith. His book *The Rapture Trap* refutes the claims made in the *Left Behind* series, explaining the origins of the mistaken and nonbiblical concept of the "secret rapture," and explaining the true Christian teachings, which reside in the Catholic Church. In part, he makes this observation about the emergence of the rapture doctrine:

"So when and how did the secret rapture notion first come about? The doctrine as it is currently taught in fundamentalist circles seems to have evolved in the nineteenth century. In the previous century, however, similar notions cropped up occasionally in colonial America.

"In the early part of the eighteenth century, for example, Increase Mather (1639-1723), a Puritan minister in Boston, wrote of Christians being 'caught up in the air' before the world was consumed by the fire of divine judgment. In 1788, a Baptist pastor and educator of Philadelphia, Morgan Edwards, published an essay promoting a similar idea, teaching that Christians would be taken to heaven three-and-a-half years before Christ judged the world. Edwards admitted in his essay that his ideas were uncommon among his peers.

"The next hint of such a doctrine appears, surprisingly enough, in the writing of a Chilean Jesuit named Manuel Lacunza. His book *The Coming of Messiah in Glory and*

Majesty was published in Spanish in 1812. In this massive volume, Lacunza concluded that toward the end of the world, Jesus would snatch up from earth the faithful believers who regularly received the Eucharist. Then the Lord would keep them safe for forty-five days while terrible judgments chastised the world. Finally, He would appear with them on earth to judge the human race. This scenario is similar to the *Left Behind* scenario, though the latter assumes that the subsequent great tribulation will last seven years instead.

"Lacunza's book was translated into English in 1827 by Edward Irving, a minister of the Protestant Church of Scotland, who was later excommunicated from his denomination for teaching that Christ's human nature was sinful. After being removed from his local congregation, he helped to organize a new denomination called the 'Catholic Apostolic Church' (which was of course neither Catholic nor Apostolic), which was in some ways a forerunner of the modern Pentecostal movement. Apparently under Lacunza's influence, Irving began preaching the secret rapture, though he, unlike Lacunza, thought it would happen three and a half years before Christ's final coming.

"About the same time, a secret coming of Christ was being preached by John Nelson Darby, a leader of the British sectarian group called the Plymouth Brethren. This group experienced numerous conflicts and schisms, some resulting from disagreements over the secret rapture teaching. Historians debate the extent to which Irving may have influenced Darby, but in any case, both 'Irvingites' and 'Darbyites' came to adopt the secret rapture teaching.

"In time, Darby traveled extensively preaching his ideas about the end times, making seven trips to Canada and the

United States alone between 1859 and 1874. His ideas began to gain acceptance at the influential 'Bible prophecy' conferences of the time, which in turn shaped the beliefs of tens of thousands of American Protestants. As a result, several popular evangelical Protestant leaders in America came under his influence, including the famous revivalist Dwight L. Moody, the shoe-salesman-turned-preacher who captivated enormous crowds of listeners on both sides of the Atlantic."[1]

Thigpen goes on to explain that Darby was especially hostile to the Catholic Church. In fact, the author of the aforementioned *Left Behind* series of books seriously pillories the Catholic Church throughout his ill-informed, misguided, and completely fictitious series of volumes.

The Catholic Church doesn't claim to know the specific meaning of all that is depicted in the Book of Revelation (also called the Apocalypse). What will actually happen at the end of time—and when that will be—is completely unknown to any human being; but we do know with certainty the outcome and who the victor will be. There are parts of Scripture that are *literal* and easy to understand, but there are also *spiritual* portions, which are cryptic and not for us to comprehend while in this world.

It seems to many theological scholars that the Apocalypse may be not only referring to future events, but it also may be talking about things that have already taken place. The Book of Revelation seems to largely be about the fall of Jerusalem, but there is no way to know this for sure.

If one only looks for it, in the last book of the New Testament you will find references to the Holy Sacrifice of the Mass and to Our Lady. In Revelation 12:1-6, it talks about the "woman and the dragon." There is no doubt that when it depicts the fact that she would give birth to a child who would "rule all nations," that child was none other than Jesus Christ, and the dragon who sought to devour that child was Satan himself.

In 2:17, the reference to a "white pebble" on which a new name is written obviously refers to the sacred Host (bread) we receive in Holy Communion. Also, if you read 7:3, 14:1, and 22:4, you will recognize the sign of the Cross. In 4:8, we read about the Holy, Holy, Holy, which we repeat at every Mass. There are several more references to the elements of the Mass we attend and assist at even today. But many of the things we read in the Apocalypse will never make sense to us while in this world.

Having said that, the author of the *Left Behind* series made assumptions and conclusions based on faulty and erroneous deductions put forth by John Nelson Darby and his predecessors who concocted the "secret rapture" scenario. Not all Protestant denominations buy into the concept of the rapture. In fact, some unbelievably claim that, because one obstinate Jesuit priest put forth a similar idea, it was the Catholics who led many Protestants astray and perpetuated this theory. But since a few Protestants came up with this theory way before the Jesuit Lacunza, that claim is ridiculous on its face.

The Catholic Church has never proffered evidence or provided any specific teaching regarding much of what is contained in the Book of Revelation (Apocalypse) up to this point. That does not mean that the Holy Spirit will never reveal its full meaning someday. Perhaps when Our Lord gets close to bringing forth the end of the world, He will make some of the things that we haven't yet understood clearer to us. It's possible that will be done in an effort to convince more people to follow Christ, thereby giving them a chance of salvation. We know without a doubt that He wants us all in heaven, but it's ultimately our choice to accept what Christ teaches through Scripture and His Church.

It is interesting that one of the aspects of the rapture theory is that faithful Christians will be spared the tribulation that the world will experience before the last day, as they will be taken to heaven before it all begins. Furthermore, the rapture believers say Jesus will be the one to come and get the true believers. In essence, that would be the Second Coming. Following that logic, at the end of the age, on the last day, when Christ comes again, that will have been His "third coming." Nowhere in Scripture or in any of the Church teachings since the time of Christ is that scenario even hinted at by anyone.

It is the opinion of the Doctors of the Church and Catholic theologians, past and present, that all those who are in the world at the time of the great trial or tribulation will experience what occurs. There may be time for many more human beings to decide to follow Christ and enter the Church, which is what God desperately wants for all His children. Does the *Catechism of the Catholic Church* suggest or posit that the Jewish people left in the world will actually realize that Jesus Christ is the Messiah before the Second Coming and enter His Holy Church? Many believe so. This is what the *Catechism* (no. 674) says:

"The glorious Messiah's coming is suspended at every moment of history until his recognition by 'all Israel,' for 'a hardening has come upon part of Israel' in their 'unbelief' toward Jesus. St. Peter says to the Jews of Jerusalem after Pentecost: 'Repent therefore, and turn again, that your sins may be blotted out, that times of refreshing may come from the presence of the

Lord, and that he may send the Christ appointed for you, Jesus, whom heaven must receive until the time for establishing all that God spoke by the mouth of his holy prophets from of old.' St. Paul echoes him: 'For if their rejection means the reconciliation of the world, what will their acceptance mean but life from the dead?' The 'full inclusion' of the Jews in the Messiah's salvation, in the wake of 'the full number of the gentiles,' will enable the People of God to achieve 'the measure of the stature of the fullness of Christ,' in which 'God may be all in all.'"

To further expand on the fact that everyone remaining on earth before the last day will experience a tribulation, or final trial, read no. 675 in the *Catechism of the Catholic Church*, which states the following:

"Before Christ's second coming, the Church must pass through a final trial that will shake the faith of many believers. The persecution that accompanies her pilgrimage on earth will unveil the 'mystery of iniquity' in the form of a religious deception offering men an apparent solution to their problems at the price of apostasy from the truth. The supreme religious deception is that of the Antichrist, a pseudo-messianism by which many glorifies himself in place of God and of his Messiah come in the flesh."

It would be wise and advisable to accept all of the teachings of the Church as they have always been and as they have gently developed with the assistance of the Holy Spirit, who has guided her in the truth throughout the ages. The bottom line is that if God chooses to reveal the full meaning of the Book of Revelation at some point, we will know it. Otherwise, probably the best course to follow is to not be highly speculative regarding the many veiled words contained in much of Scripture, and especially in the Apocalypse.

Let's cherish our Catholic identity and not be taken in by the wanderings in the faith and the imaginative theories being brought forth by non-Catholics—and indeed wayward Catholic clergy and laypeople—who possess faulty biblical and theological knowledge.

Chapter 12
Marriage, the Family, and Sexual Morality:
Changing Attitudes

In the modern world, we as a people have become so educated and enlightened, apparently, that what God laid out for us regarding marriage, having a family, and sexual morality is now said to be old-fashioned. Many believe we have to change our thinking and accept and honor things that have heretofore been considered evil and morally corrupt. After all, God is a loving God and He will accept anything we do as long as we don't hurt someone else in the process. He is all-merciful and, as a result of that, everyone will eventually end up in heaven. Does this attitude sound familiar?

It is unfortunate that these terribly erroneous sentiments pervade much of the modern thought in our Holy Catholic Church. To many members of the clergy and laypeople, same-sex marriage is now acceptable because, after all, if two men or two women love each other, that can only be good. Love is all that is important, and God teaches us to love one another. Never mind that this conclusion is not biblical and has never been Church teaching.

Many, many, "married" same-sex couples are adopting children. Laws are being made that not only protect adoption agencies who allow this, but they make it possible to sue

Catholic adoption agencies that will not allow it; thus, many of the Catholic agencies have had to close—or be sued. There is evidence, according to hundreds of psychiatrists and psychologists, that being raised in a same-sex parent environment can be very detrimental to a child's mental health. Some believe that depression, suicide, and other problems are much more prevalent among children raised by gay or lesbian parents. You can also find studies that purport that the opposite is true—that the children inserted into these families fare no worse than the ones with both a father and a mother.

It's not hard to deduct that the results of these studies most likely reflect the personal beliefs and views of the people or organizations conducting the them. What we as Catholics—and indeed all Christians—need to do is rely on the perennial teachings of Christ and His Holy Church. Morality doesn't change according to the way the wind blows at a particular time in history.

I will briefly say that the issue of transgenderism is so far from God's plan that it boggles the mind. To actually believe that Our Lord made a mistake when He created an individual is beyond comprehension, but as a society we are now accepting it as normal more and more every day. Many people think and say that a mere child can decide to change his or her gender. Is that a lucid and valid conclusion? For an adult parent to feed into and even support this unnatural idea and then help to facilitate that actually happening is extremely twisted; it is without a doubt child abuse.

The problems I have just outlined, although not exclusive, come from a perversion of Catholic teaching that has taken place over many decades due to the modernist ideology that has become popular with both wayward clergy and laypeople. It is important to refresh the minds of misled Catholics regarding what is, and always has been, Church teaching about marriage and families.

I will be quoting extensively from the *Precis of Official Catholic Teaching* and the volume on marriage, family, and sexuality. This work, which is predicated upon, and faithful to, the *Catechism of the Catholic Church* and Sacred Scripture, consists of thirteen volumes. It makes clear and summarizes what has always been, and always will be, what the Church teaches in this very crucial area of human life: Christian marriage.

Pope Saint John Paul II was very concerned about what was happening to the sacrament of marriage in the world and the breakdown of family life in general. The escalation in the number of divorces and adultery, due to the abysmal teaching and passing on of the faith, prompted him to compose a Post-Synodal Apostolic Exhortation, which came out on November 22, 1981. In the beginning, the following statement is put forth:

"Background: The 1980 Synod of Bishops had studied the family in the modern world. In *Familiaris Consortio,* Pope John Paul II responds to concerns raised at the Synod with the most complete treatment of the family in any magisterial document. In nn. 28-35, he reaffirms the teaching of *Humana Vitae* in a personalist way. In 1981, the crucial year of the attempt on his life, the Pope also established the Pontifical Council for the Family in the Curia and the first Pontifical Institute for the Family in Rome."[1]

When we procreate as Catholics, the children we are blessed with not only deserve our love and physical care, we are to be concerned with their development as Christians. The former pope wrote this:

"The Christian family is the first community called to announce the Gospel to the human person during growth and to bring him or her through progressive education and catechesis, to full human and Christian maturity."[2]

We as Christian parents bear a great responsibility on behalf of Christ and for the spiritual good of our children, who will do the same one day when they become parents.

"The Church is deeply convinced that only by the acceptance of the Gospel are the hopes that man legitimately places in marriage and in the family capable of being fulfilled.

"... When the family is the object of numerous forces that seek to destroy or deform it, the Church perceives in a more urgent and compelling way her mission of proclaiming to all people the plan of God for marriage and the family"[3]

For many, many years, for some reason, bishops and priests of the Catholic Church have been negligent in passing on the strict and immutable teachings of the faith in general. There is ample evidence to indicate that in an effort to be more "ecumenical" and "nicer," they in essence watered down the "rules" to be more like Protestant denominations. This effort has led to countless problems which the Church has encountered over the last fifty or sixty years, including the acceptance by the faithful of abortion, contraception, and euthanasia. Also, the lack of belief in the Real Presence of Christ in the Eucharist has caused a mass exodus of millions of Catholics who have left to join the Protestant ranks. Since Catholics could no longer perceive a difference in their church and the tens of thousands of Protestant denominations, why not join a church where you can enjoy a concert and drink coffee during the services.

When it comes to the Christian responsibility of pastors, the *Precis* repeats this quote of Pope John Paul II:

"The pastors must promote the sense of the faith in all the faithful, examine and authoritatively judge the genuineness of its expressions and educate the faithful in an ever more mature evangelical discernment....

"At the root of negative phenomena (e.g., divorce, abortion, a contraceptive mentality), there frequently lies a corruption of the idea and the experience of freedom, conceived not as a capacity for realizing the truth of God's plan for marriage and the family, but as an autonomous power of self-affirmation, often against others, for one's own selfish well-being....

"Society must be renewed to the point of recapturing the ultimate meaning of life and its fundamental values."[4]

In an effort to further explain the importance and real meaning of marriage, Pope Saint John Paul II put it this way:

"The communion of love between God and people finds a meaningful expression in the marriage covenant established between a man and woman.

"Their bond of love becomes the image and the symbol of the covenant which unites God and His people....

"The marriage of baptized persons thus becomes a real symbol of that new and eternal covenant sanctioned in the blood of Christ....

"By virtue of the sacramentality of their marriage, spouses are bound to one another in the most profoundly indissoluble manner, their belonging to each other is the real representation, by means of the sacramental sign, of the very relationship of Christ with the Church."[5]

It seems that the sacrament of marriage has been devalued not only due to ignorance of the faith, but by an acceptance by most of the world that if problems cannot be worked out, or if you get tired of your spouse, you can just get divorced and move on. It's very sad that over 50 percent of marriages in the United States end up in divorce, and many of those are Catholic marriages. That sentimentality on the part of Catholics prompted the saintly pope to teach us this:

"Conjugal communion is characterized not only by its unity, but also by its indissolubility.

"As a mutual gift of two persons, this intimate union, as well as the good of children, imposes total fidelity on the spouses and argues for an unbreakable oneness between them.

"God wills and communicates the indissolubility of marriage as a fruit, a sign, and a requirement of the absolutely faithful love that God has for man and that Lord Jesus has for the Church."[6]

Addressing the specific and ecclesial role of families, we would do well to internalize and accept the following statement of our former pope:

"The Christian family is called upon to place itself in what is and what it does as an 'intimate community of life and love' at the service of Church and society.

"The family's sharing in the Church's mission must be 'of one heart and soul' (Acts 4:32) in faith through shared apostolic zeal and shared commitment to works of service in the ecclesial and civil communities.

"It is in the love between husband and wife and between the members of the family that the Christian family's participation in the prophetic, priestly, and kingly mission of Jesus Christ and His Church finds expression and realization.

"Love and life thus constitute the nucleus of the saving mission of the Christian family in and for the Church."[7]

When it comes to serving the Church, the following is very instructive and Important to remember:

"The ministry of evangelization carried out by Christian parents is original and irreplaceable.

"The family must educate the children for life in such a way that each one may fully perform his or her role according to the vocation received from God.

"The parent's ministry of evangelization and catechesis ought to play a part in their children's lives also during adolescence and youth, when the children challenge or even reject the Christian faith received in earlier years.

"It should not be forgotten that the service rendered by Christian spouses and parents to the Gospel is essentially an ecclesial service."[8]

We find in these very wise words that the Source and Summit of our Catholic faith applies very directly to the sacrament of marriage and the Christian family:

"The Christian family's sanctifying role is grounded in baptism and has its highest expression in the Eucharist, to which Christian marriage is intimately connected.

"The Eucharist is the very source of Christian marriage.

"In this sacrifice of the new and eternal covenant, Christian spouses encounter the source from which their own

marriage covenant flows, is interiorly structured and continuously renewed.

"The Eucharist is a foundation of charity, and in the
Eucharistic gift of charity the Christian family finds the foundation and soul of its 'communion' and its 'mission.'"9

Pope Saint John Paul II sets forth the importance of prayer
among family members. Of course, the responsibility of making
this happen falls on the parents. These are his exhortations on
this subject:

"The baptismal priesthood of the faithful exercised in the
sacrament of marriage constitutes the basis of a priestly vocation and mission for spouses and family by which their daily
lives are transformed onto spiritual sacrifices acceptable to God
through Jesus Christ.

"It is prayer offered in common, husband and wife
together, parents and children together, which is both a conse-
quence of and a requirement for the communion bestowed by
the sacraments of baptism and matrimony.

"Family prayer has for its very own object family life itself,
which is seen as a call from God and lived as a filial response to
His call.

"The dignity and responsibility of the Christian family as
the domestic church can be achieved only with God's unceasing
aid, which will surely be granted if it is humbly and trustingly
petitioned in prayer."10

Again, emphasizing that parents are really the ones who
have the most influence on their children when it comes to
passing on the faith, Pope Saint John Paul II puts it this way:

"The Christian family, enriched by the grace and the office
of the sacrament of matrimony, must teach the children from

the earliest age, according to the faith received in baptism, to have a knowledge of God, to worship Him and to love their neighbor.

"The concrete example and living witness of parents is fundamental and irreplaceable in educating their children to pray.

"In his appeal to parents, Pope Paul VI said: 'your example of honesty in thought and action, joined in some common prayer, is a lesson for life, an act of worship of singular value. In this way, you bring peace to your homes: *Pax huic domui*. Remember, it is thus that you build up the Church' (General Audience Aug. 11, 1976; *Insegnamenti di Paolo VI,* 14 (1976) (640)."[11]

In today's modern society, it is all too common for both young and mature couples to make the decision to simply live together until they can decide whether marriage is the right move for them. They justify their decision to do so in many different ways: maybe it's cheaper to occupy one apartment or house; the couple can live together in order to find out if they are compatible with each other; they can decide whether they make good sexual partners, and on and on—you get the point. Many modern couples who live together just have no intention of getting married because, after all, the marriage "certificate" is just a piece of paper, so why bother making it legal. That way, when one gets tired of, or mad at, the other, they can simply make a clean break—no messy divorce or hiring a lawyer to split up the "stuff."

Countless Catholics who don't understand their faith, and therefore don't see marriage as the sacrament and Christian vocation that it is meant to be, are participating in what the

Church calls "trial marriages" more and more these days. And while they do this, they attend Mass and receive Holy Communion, not realizing what they are doing is sinful—as it always has been—according to the Catholic Church.

Pope Saint John Paul II had this to say on the subjects of "irregular situations" and "trial marriages":

"The Synod of Bishops took careful consideration of certain situations which are irregular in a religious sense and often in the civil sense.

"Such situations are widespread among Catholics with no little damage to the family and society, of which the family is the basic cell.

"A first example of an irregular situation is 'trial marriages.' Human reason leads one to see that they are unacceptable by showing the unconvincing nature of carrying out an experiment with human beings whose dignity demands they should be always and solely the term of self-giving love without limitation of time or of any other circumstance.

"The Church for her part cannot admit such a kind of union for further and original reasons which derive from faith.

"In the first place, the gift of the body in the sexual relationship is a real symbol of the giving of the whole person.

"Such giving cannot take place with full truth without the concourse of the love of charity, given by Christ.

"In the second place, marriage between two baptized persons is a real symbol of the union of Christ and the Church, which is not a temporary 'trial union.'

"Such a situation cannot usually be overcome unless the person from childhood, with the help of Christ's grace and without fear, has been trained to dominate concupiscence from the beginning to establish relationships of genuine love with other people.

"It will be very useful to investigate the causes of this phenomena, including its psychological and sociological aspects, in order to find a remedy.

"*De facto free unions:*

"This means unions without any publicly recognized institutional bond, either civil or religious.

"Some people consider themselves almost forced into a free union by difficult economic, cultural, or religious situations.

"In other cases, one encounters people who scorn, rebel against, or reject society, and the institution of the family, and are only seeking pleasure.

"Each of these elements presents the Church with arduous pastoral problems by reason of the serious consequences deriving from them, both religious and moral.

"The pastors and the ecclesial community should take care to become acquainted with such situations and their causes, case by case.

"The people of God should approach the public authorities in order that they may resist these tendencies which divide society and are harmful to the dignity, security, and welfare of the citizens as individuals.

"Society and the public authorities should favor legitimate marriage by means of a series of social and political actions which will guarantee a family wage by issuing directives ensuring housing fitting for family life and by creating opportunities for work and life.

"*Catholics in civil marriages.*

"There are increasing cases of Catholics who for ideological or practical reasons prefer to contract a merely civil marriage and who reject, or at least defer, religious marriage.

"The aim of pastoral action will be to make these people understand the need for consistency between their choice of life and the faith they profess and to try to do everything possible to induce them to regularize their situation in the light of Christian principles."[12]

It is long past time for pastoral clarifications on the sacrament of marriage, cohabitation, contraception, and family life from our bishops and priests. We can no longer afford to keep the Church's teachings on these very important subjects locked away in the archives, papal documents, and canon law. We as Catholics should have priests who are not afraid to preach the unadulterated truth from the pulpit. Why do you think many Catholics—especially the young ones—don't even know where the Church stands in these matters? It's because, for many inexplicable and insufficient reasons, these subjects have been avoided in the nice-sounding, toothless platitudes we often hear in modern-day homilies.

In order to restore our true Catholic identity, Catholics must know and understand these things that have been ignored for so long, and bishops and priests must man up and begin to teach the truth once again.

Chapter 13
Catholic Charismatic Renewal

There is a phenomenon within the Catholic Church that exists and has become very popular since Vatican II, which eventually came to be called the Charismatic Renewal. This movement stemmed from a Protestant movement that began during the so-called Reformation in the early sixteenth century.

Here again, since the spirit of the Second Vatican Council was heavily encouraging a new kind of ecumenism, many Catholics—including bishops and priests—thought it appropriate to join with the Protestants and adopt some of their methods of worship. This type of "ecumenism" was another in the long line of diversions from true Catholicism and a desire on the part of some to find a "new way" to strengthen one's faith, but it was all based on a flawed interpretation of Scripture—the Protestant interpretation.

In the early 1900s, several of the Protestant denominations existing at the time had broken into different groups because of their disagreement regarding their theories about how the Holy Spirit externally manifests Himself in the lives of individuals. Even now, Protestant denominations split off to form other versions that will agree with their own doctrines on any given subject.

Many Catholics who have involved themselves in the Charismatic Renewal believe this "new" manifestation and "outpouring" of the Holy Spirit is an additional dimension that should be added to the Catholic Church's type of worship. It is another example of believing new programs need to continually be added to the Church Jesus Christ gave us; somehow the old program is not good enough for the modern times we live in, and to keep Catholics' attention and help them grow in their faith, we need to keep trying different approaches.

Pentecostalism—the Charismatic Renewal—is symptomatic of the need and desire of poorly catechized Catholics to strengthen their faith and get closer to Our Lord; that is the good news. If they had been taught and learned the true faith well to begin with, they wouldn't be looking for other ways to get closer to God. When one is confused in the faith, it is natural to seek certainty about it. People can't be blamed for seeking a closer relationship with Christ, that's for sure. But there are problems with Pentecostalism in that inconsistencies and inaccuracies exist in their methods.

It can be deduced that many people who seek out and become involved in the Charismatic Renewal are infants in the faith. In other words, they probably don't really know what the Church teaches and are ignorant of the riches the Church has always possessed (and I don't mean monetary riches). Many of those involved in this movement actually come to challenge the Church's authority in some instances, and the methods they employ sometimes can even become dangerous to the soul. I think we can infer that the Holy Spirit would not contradict Himself and His Church, right? Some of the people (I don't want to generalize and lump them all together) involved in

Pentecostalism forsake Catholic devotions like the rosary, veneration of Mary and sacred statues, adoration, novenas, etc., to concentrate on the gifts of the Holy Spirit—who they sometimes seem to forget is part of the Holy Trinity.

The gifts of the Holy Spirit they focus on most are the ability to speak in tongues and the act of being "baptized in the Spirit." Speaking in tongues is a subject that is widely misunderstood.

On the subject of speaking in tongues, I will relate a story I know of personally. A very dear friend of mine got involved in a Pentecostal group back in the 1970s while in college. She grew up Catholic in a large devout family. Most of the people in her group were Protestants, but not all. She and the other young Catholics began attending a Protestant church. After a few years being involved, my friend returned to the Catholic Church. In a discussion with her, I inquired about the whole situation. She divulged to me that for some time it felt like there was a lot of insincerity, acting, and deception in what the charismatics were saying and doing. I asked her if she had ever spoken in tongues. Her answer to me was that she tried doing it and, in fact, thought she was doing it. The concept as explained to her was just to make noises, not speaking in any real language, and the Holy Spirit would know you were praying and be pleased. She did that over and over but began questioning the efficacy of the act. She told me, "How can I be praying when I don't even know what I'm saying?" Speaking in tongues seemed to be their main focus, although they did pray as a group, trying to invoke the Holy Spirit.

According to Pentecostalism/Charismatic Renewal, one can become an immediate mystic. We are to believe that the gift of tongues has now been conferred on the hundreds of thousands—maybe millions—who are part of this movement, even though very few during Apostolic times and in the following 2,000 years received that special gift. Men such as Saint John of the Cross warned Catholics of the possible harm that can come from actively pursuing such gifts, indicating that they could be open to being deceived by the devil or one's own imagination. Also, people get so immersed in this movement that it can become an excessive attachment.

The fact that the Catholic Church has approved of and supported the Charismatic Renewal is disturbing to many, including me. Some say that being involved with this kind of spirituality can prove to be just a brief time in one's spiritual journey and his or her growth as Christians, so what harm can it do. But believing you can pray for and receive the gifts of speaking in tongues and prophesy is foreign to anything in Church history.

Regarding the subject of speaking in tongues, professed by those inside the Pentecostal/Charismatic Renewal movement, I will quote portions of an article by Nathan Busenitz, written in 2006, entitled, *The Gift of Tongues: Comparing the Church Fathers with Contemporary Pentecostalism*. Speaking about the nature of tongues-speaking, he says this:

"In spite of a relative de-emphasis placed on tongues-speaking by the church fathers (who speak of prophecy much more than they do of tongues), they are not altogether silent on the issue. In fact, their collective writings overwhelmingly suggest that they associate tongues-speaking with a supernatural ability to speak rational, authentic foreign languages. That proposition is directly supported by Irenaeus, Hippolytus, Hegemonius, Gregory of Nazianzen, Ambrosiaster, Chrysostom,

Augustine, Leo the Great, and implied by others (such as Tertullian and Origen). Such a proposition is further strengthened by the fathers' equation of the Acts 2 use of the gift with the Corinthian phenomenon (as well as their allusions to Isaiah 28:11 where discussing the NT gift)....

"Thus, the patristic evidence supports a rational foreign language as the proper and normal manifestation of tongues. Conversely, unintelligible babblings and irrational gibberish are never associated with the gift."[1]

It's clear when reading Church history that very few were ever given the gift of speaking in tongues. Any special gift of the Holy Spirit is only given to very holy and prayerful individuals, not because they asked for that gift, but because God in his divine beneficence affords it. On that very subject, Dr. Busenitz had this to say:

"The church fathers also viewed tongues-speaking as a supernatural gift. No amount of human exertion, initiation, or training could aid in acquiring what was endowed only by the Holy Spirit."[2]

Later in his extensive article, Nathan Busenitz refers to Saint Paul's Epistles, and specifically 1-2 Corinthians and concluded the following:

"Paul is emphatic in asserting that the distribution of gifts is not to be attributed to human causes as if they were achievable by men. The varied gifts of the Holy Spirit and the grace of the Lord Jesus are the work of one and the same God.

"Thus, the gifts (including tongues) did not involve any prior human effort or ability to attain."[3]

Another thing regarding speaking in tongues is that the Church has always taught that when tongues were spoken, the ability for translation is necessary for the edification of the Church; otherwise, it is unprofitable. That also implies that a type of speech that is not interpreted or understood by anyone could be of questionable—even diabolical—origin.

The Charismatic Renewal/Pentecostal movement is simply not of the Church Jesus Christ gave us. We would do well as Catholics to stick with the immutable teachings passed down to us from Christ through the Apostles and His Bride, His Holy Catholic Church. To get caught up in and to be enthralled by every new program and movement that comes along would be a mistake. If we only learn our faith more completely and immerse ourselves in the Mass, prayer, adoration, and all of the great and rich traditions that have always been with us, our faith will grow stronger, and our true Catholic identity will be restored.

Chapter 14

Would Jesus Support Socialism?

It is an unfortunate fact that many Catholics are of the opinion that socialism is more in line with what Jesus taught than is capitalism, which is the system we've had in the United States from our beginning. The socialist/communist ideology has failed everywhere in the world it has been tried. Some other countries are also moving in this failed direction.

The reason people are being drawn to socialism in the United States is similar to the reason Catholics have gone astray from the Church's teachings, and that is a widespread ignorance of history. In fact, much of the history taught in high schools and universities is a revisionist version. A political bias is driving this perversion of the truth by liberal academics who are trying to sway and influence students in one direction—their direction—whether it contains the truth or not. At the time of this writing, historical statues are being torn down by rioters in many cities around the country. Liberal politicians are now ordering statues to be removed as they succumb to the demands of those who do not understand that we cannot erase our history, good or bad, and think that will make things better. Both the triumphs and the mistakes in our history must be remembered if we are to avoid doing the wrong things over again.

Americans in general, many of whom are Catholic, now support politicians with socialist tendencies who want to fundamentally change the country of our Christian founders—all based on a flawed idea of what Christians should desire for mankind. It is thought that most of the Americans who lean toward socialism are millennials (those becoming adults in the early 21st century). That may be true because of the increased efforts by schools, teachers, and professors to promote a socialist agenda. But as in the case of Church teaching and its history being watered down over many decades, older Americans have never learned what a true and complete history of our country entails. They are being led by the nose by unscrupulous politicians, for the most part, and the American way of life is being threatened like never before.

The proponents of socialism paint a rosy picture of what it would be like if everyone was economically equal in every possible way. They believe owning more property than one's neighbor is somehow wrong and unjust; earning more money than someone else because of one's own initiative to improve his or her financial condition is not just; and creating a "utopia" in which all people are economically equal in every way would cure the ills of society.

The main problem with socialism and communism is that the ideas contained in these ideologies are not only wrong in their desired outcome, they are anti-Christian. Scripture bears that out if one only looks for it. The problems in the world are much more in the spiritual realm than the worldly one. As Christians, we must realize that the suffering that occurs in the world is due to sin. Nothing that we as human beings do will rid the world of suffering. We must live to love and serve Our Lord, pray for and help others, and live our lives in a way that will please Him. There is nothing in Scripture that teaches we must strive to be equal in every possible way during our lives. Every human being has equal love and dignity from Jesus Christ, there is no doubt about that.

The Bible emphasizes individual responsibility when it comes to working and providing for oneself and his or her family.

"And whoever does not provide for relatives and especially family members has denied the faith and is worse than an unbeliever" (1 Timothy 5:8).

Unfortunately, there are those in society who believe they are owed a living by the government, meaning that all citizens must pay for them to exist. What does Scripture say about that? In Saint Paul's second letter to the Thessalonians, a clear and unambiguous statement was made in this matter:

"In fact, when we were with you, we instructed you that if anyone was unwilling to work, neither should that one eat" (2 Thessalonians 3:10).

There are several other passages in the Bible that make it crystal clear that we all have a personal responsibility to make our own way the best we can while in the world. Yes, we have a Christian responsibility to help our fellow human beings when they are suffering or in need, but the choice to do so rests on us as individuals, according to our ability. It should not be the prerogative of any government to forcibly take money or property from any citizen to give to another citizen, whatever their perceived reason may be. Consider that doing so is a violation of the Seventh Commandment, which teaches us "you shall not steal." In other words, the government would be taking something which is not theirs from someone to give to another. That's stealing.

Remember, we in the United States elect our representatives in free and fair elections. Therefore, as our founders envisioned, "We the People" are the ultimate deciders of how things work, but we have a Constitution to guide us in that effort. More and more, wayward politicians are attempting to sidestep and avoid the tenets of that Constitution in order to fundamentally change the United States of America. The fact that many Americans are letting them get away with it because of their ignorance of history and of the failed results of socialism and communism around the world, I find it disconcerting to say the least. It would behoove Catholics to revisit those instructive portions in Scripture regarding these moral issues, and all Americans should study the history of socialism in the world in order to garner the actual facts about that very flawed system of government. The bottom line is that socialism is not a Catholic concept in any way, shape, or form, and implementing this system in America would be very detrimental to faith, family, and all individuals' natural rights.

To become a socialist would be to cease to be Catholic. Let's return to our true Catholic identity—the one that embraces the actual teachings of the Church and recognizes the Christian principles that we should have been taught through the Church and in our history classes over the years. And let's hold our elected officials accountable for what they advocate for, while serving at our pleasure.

Chapter 15

Artificial Insemination, Abortion, and Euthanasia

Over the years, confusion has come about regarding many of the moral choices Catholics must make during their lifetimes. Due to weak, and indeed erroneous, teachings by many bishops and priests in the Church, it has been difficult to discern what is and is not forbidden for Catholics. Three of the areas of confusion are artificial insemination, abortion, and euthanasia. As Catholics, we must understand that all three of these acts are, in fact, grave sins.

In my discourse on these subjects, I will again consult the *Precis of Official Catholic Teaching,* which is a Church-approved summary of Church teaching that is contained in thirteen volumes.

First, I will quote parts of Pope Pius XII's address to the Fourth International Congress of Catholic Doctors on Artificial Insemination, given on September 29, 1949. The pope expressly rejected the insemination of women in two ways: with sperm provided by a donor outside of marriage (AID), and sperm provided by the husband (AIH). It is important to note that thirty-eight years later, in *Donum Vitae,* the Congregation for the Doctrine of the Faith, with the approval of then-Pope John Paul II, applied the very same principles.

After making the case that Christian doctors must use their knowledge and talents to preserve their patients' health and help bring about healing when possible, it was also stated that the doctors must abide by Christian morals and ethics in practicing their profession. In the natural course of human life, the Church teaches that there are certain lines that must not be crossed. The Church also emphasizes that those in the medical profession cannot attempt to play God and delve into very questionable areas. Ultimately, only God has dominion over one's life and destiny. One of the dangerous areas many in the medical profession have promoted is artificial insemination, and this is what was said in this address to Catholic doctors:

"Another pressing problem has now arisen that demands the light of Catholic moral doctrine: the problem of artificial insemination.

"When dealing with man, the question of artificial insemination cannot be considered either exclusively, nor yet principally, under its biological and medical aspect, leaving aside the moral and juridical point of view.

"Artificial insemination outside matrimony must be condemned as immoral, purely and simply.

In fact, the natural law and the divine positive law state that the procreation of new life cannot take place except in marriage.

"Only matrimony safeguards the dignity of the partners—in the present case principally that of the woman—and their personal well-being, and guarantees at the same time the well-being of the child and his upbringing.

"It follows that there cannot be any difference of opinion among Catholics regarding the condemnation of artificial insemination outside the conjugal union.

"Artificial insemination in matrimony, but produced by means of the active element of a third person, is equally immoral and as such is to be condemned without right of appeal.

"Only the husband and wife have the reciprocal right to the body of the other for the purpose of generating new life: an exclusive, inalienable, incommunicable right."[1]

Regarding the legitimacy of artificial insemination, this was what was told to Catholic doctors:

"Let it suffice to recall these principles of the natural law: the mere fact that the means reaches the goal intended does not justify the use of the means.

"Nor does the desire for a child suffice to prove that recourse to artificial fecundation is legitimate because it would satisfy such a desire.

"It would be mistaken to consider that the possibility of resorting to this means could render valid a marriage between persons incapable of contracting it because of the impediment of impotency.

"The active element can never be licitly procured by acts against nature.

"Though new methods cannot be excluded *a priori* simply because they are new, in the case of artificial insemination, one must exclude it altogether."[2]

In November of 1974, the Congregation for the Doctrine of the Faith (CDF) put forth a *Declaration on Procured Abortion*, which began as follows:

"The great moral issue which emerged in the late sixties was abortion. Due to pressure from secularist and radical feminist groups, many nations legalized procured abortion in the seventies and eighties. The Second Vatican Council denounced abortion as an 'unspeakable crime' (*Gaudium et Spes,* n. 51), a judgment in accord with classical Christian tradition since the earliest times. This declaration became the point of reference for the thousands of Catholic men and women who, united with other Christians and people of good will, continue to struggle in various ways to protect the right to life of the unborn."[3]

There is a document on Christian teaching, written by the early bishops of the Church, called the Didache (pronounced did-a-kay). Expert historians and theologians believe that some of the Apostles contributed to its authorship because the first iteration was offered between AD 50 and 70. It is believed that additions were made over many years as the Church grew and expanded on many of the teachings.

These words appear in the Didache:

"You shall not kill the fetus by abortion and you shall not murder the infant already born."

The CDF also wrote this in their *Declaration on Procured Abortion*:

"Tertullian clearly affirms the essential principle: 'To prevent birth is anticipated murder; it makes little difference whether one destroys a life already born or does away with it in its nascent stage. The one who will be a man is already one.'

"The various opinions on the infusion of the spiritual soul did not introduce any doubt about the illicitness of abortion.

"Although medieval authors had diverse opinions regarding the infusion of a spiritual soul, it was never denied that procured abortion, even during the first days, was objectively a grave fault. This condemnation was, in fact, unanimous.

"The first Council of Mainz in 847 decided that the most rigorous penance would be imposed 'on women who procure the elimination of the fruit conceived in their womb.'"[4]

Considering all of the confusion and problems emanating from Vatican II, the CDF made this statement:

"The Second Vatican Council has most severely condemned abortion: 'Life must be safeguarded with extreme care from conception; abortion and infanticide are abominable crimes.'"[5]

The complete writing of the aforementioned Didache is widely available for anyone to read, if one has a desire to do so. It is plain to see, read, and understand that abortion has always been a grave sin committed by a doctor who performs one, by the women and men who seek and obtain one, by politicians who pass laws allowing this heinous act, and by individuals who vote for and support those politicians.

In years past, most Catholics understood this important teaching, which simply comes from the Commandment "Thou shalt not kill." Many Catholics have fallen victim to the worldly, secular belief that killing a human being in the uterus is somehow acceptable in the modern world. These misguided Catholics have lost their identity, but it's never too late to repent and come back to the truth.

We will now discuss Church teaching on euthanasia, another grave act that is garnering acceptance in the world, supported by wayward Catholics. The merciless killing of the elderly is being championed by the population control advocates in the name of being "kind and merciful" to the sick. This is another example of a certain group of individuals trying to play God and decide who should live or die, and when they should do it.

The Catholic Church, again, has always opposed this very non-Christian Idea. In 1980, the Congregation for the Doctrine of the Faith made a declaration on euthanasia. It began as follows:

"Euthanasia, or 'good death,' is the 'mercy-killing' of gravely ill, aged or mentally defective persons. By claiming that some lives are of less value than others, euthanasia draws on the same logic and pagan anthropology which justifies and promotes abortion. Delayed in reaction to Nazi 'mercy-killing,' attempts to legalize euthanasia were gradually revived as memories of that shameful era faded. Alert to this new menace and with the approval of Pope Paul VI, the Congregation for the Doctrine of the Faith confronts euthanasia. In the last decades of the Twentieth Century, pro-life Christians continue to fight attempts to legalize this second great threat to the right to life."[6]

The Catholic Church has always taught that crimes against life, such as any murder, genocide, abortion, euthanasia, or willful suicide, are to be condemned and considered grave sin. We as Catholics are obligated as Christians to oppose all of these evil acts. If we do not, and if we decide to accept one or all of them, we are only fooling ourselves when we identify as Christians.

In a clear message on euthanasia, the CDF said this:

"No one has the right to kill the innocent, whether fetus, embryo, infant, adult, old person, one suffering from an incurable disease, or a dying person.

"No one is permitted to ask for such killing either for himself, herself, or for one entrusted to his or her care.

"No authority can legitimately recommend, permit, or sanction such killing.

"The pleas of gravely ill people who sometimes ask for death are not to be understood as implying a true desire for euthanasia, but in most cases constitute an anguished plea for help and love.

"What a sick person needs besides medical care is love of family, friends, doctors and nurses.

"Physical suffering is unavoidable, but it has a special place in God's saving plan.

"It is in fact a sharing in Christ's passion and a union with the redeeming sacrifice which He offered in obedience to the Father's will.

"Human and Christian prudence suggest for the majority of sick people the use of medicines capable of alleviating or suppressing pain, even though these may cause semiconsciousness and reduced lucidity.

"The use of narcotics as pain killers, if no intention of death is intended, is permissible."[7]

In all matters regarding human life, we must adhere to the revealed plan of the Creator. Those in the medical field are permitted to keep a dying or suffering person comfortable as best they can, but to end one's life in what some call an "act of mercy or charity" is unacceptable in any way, shape, or form. All Catholics must be aware of the Church's teaching on this very misunderstood subject. The true meaning of the words "mercy" and "charity" has been hijacked and misused much like the term "social justice" has been assigned a "new meaning." We must be careful not to get caught up in evil actions dressed up in sweet, nice-sounding language; that is a tactic of Satan. We all need to possess a healthy portion of skepticism regarding moral questions. The teachings of the Church are easy to find in the *Catechism of the Catholic Church*, on many Catholic websites, and in Scripture. To maintain our true Catholic identify, we must know these important lessons.

Chapter 16

A Crisis in the Priesthood

I will begin this chapter with the proclamation that there are many good and faithful cardinals, bishops, and priests in the world, to whom we should be very grateful. After all, their mission is to be "other Christs" in the world, and to pass on to us what Christ taught and revealed to the Church. Theirs is a monumental task to be sure, and their responsibility is extremely important for the salvation of souls. We need to love and support our good priests however we can. Many are fighting an uphill battle against the strong forces of evil existing in the world, but if we help them, stand behind them, and support them in their faithful efforts on behalf of Jesus and His Church, we can make their work easier.

The unfortunate news is that good, orthodox, solid Catholic priests are hard to find in some places. We can put the blame for that situation squarely on the failure of a lot of seminaries that have imparted a distorted version of the faith—even heresy—to unsuspecting seminarians. Many of these seminaries have been run by modernist instructors who have intentionally taught all kinds of error and mistaken ideas about what the essence of a priest's ministry should be. Seminaries in some places have been hotbeds of homosexual activity. There are accounts that have surfaced over the years describing how seminarians were threatened to be expelled if they didn't submit to the sexual advances of their superiors. It is thought that we have probably lost many future good priests because of their refusal to be used as sexual objects. Earlier in this book, I described how the Church was infiltrated by homosexual men and others who weren't really believers, in an effort to destroy the Church. We still have many of those evil men within the Church who continue their attempts to change Church teaching in many areas. We must be vigilant and not let them get away with it.

In February of 2020, the *National Catholic Register* published an article of an interview by the astute Catholic journalist Edward Pentin. The subject of the interview was the publication of a recent book co-written by Cardinal Robert Sarah and Pope Emeritus Benedict XVI, titled, *From the Depths of Our Hearts: Priesthood, Celibacy and the Crisis of the Catholic Church.* Cardinal Sarah was the prefect of the Congregation for Divine Worship and the Discipline of the Sacraments from November 2014 to February 2021. I will quote parts of this enlightening interview.

Mr. Pentin asked His Eminence this question:

"Your Eminence, why did you want to write this book?

"Because the Christian priesthood is in mortal danger! It's going through a major crisis.

"The discovery of the great number of sexual abuses committed by priests, and even bishops, is an indisputable symptom of this. Pope Emeritus Benedict XVI had already spoken out strongly on this subject. But then his thinking was distorted and ignored. Just like today, attempts have been made to silence him. And like today, diversionary maneuvers were mounted to divert attention from his prophetic message. Yet, I am convinced that he has told us the essential—what no one wants to hear. He has shown that at the root of the abuses committed by clerics, there is a deep flaw in their formation. The priest is a man set apart for the service of God and the Church. He is a consecrated person. His whole life is set apart for God. And yet they wanted to desacralize priestly life. They wanted to trivialize it, to render it profane, to secularize it. They wanted to make the priest a man like any other. Some priests were formed without putting God, prayer, the celebration of Mass, the ardent search for holiness at the center of their lives.

"As Benedict said, 'Why has pedophilia reached such proportions? In the final analysis, the reason is the absence of God. It is only where Faith no longer determines man's actions that such crimes are possible.'

"Precisely how poor has this formation been that you mention, and what have been the effects?

"Priests have been formed without teaching them that God is the only point of support for their lives, without making them experience that their lives only have meaning through God and for Him. Deprived of God, they were left with nothing but power. Some have fallen into the diabolical logic of abuse of authority and sexual crimes. If a priest doesn't daily experience he is only an instrument in God's hands, if he doesn't stand constantly before God to serve him with all his heart, then he risks becoming intoxicated with a sense of power. If a priest's life is not a consecrated life, then he is in great danger of illusion and diversion.

"Today, some would like to take a further step in this direction. They would like to relativize the celibacy of priests. That would be a catastrophe! For celibacy is the most obvious manifestation that the priest belongs to Christ and that he no longer belongs to himself. Celibacy is the sign of a life that has meaning only through God and for Him. To want to ordain married men is to imply that priestly life is not full time, that it does not require a complete gift, that it leaves one free for other commitments such as a profession, that it leaves time free for a private life. But this is false. A priest remains a priest at all times. Priestly ordination is not first of all a generous commitment; it is a consecration of our whole being, an indelible conformation of our soul to Christ, the priest, who demands from us permanent conversion in order to correspond to Him. Celibacy is the unquestionable sign that being a priest supposes allowing oneself to be entirely possessed by God. To call it into question would seriously aggravate the crisis of the priesthood.

"Does Pope Emeritus Benedict XVI share this point of view?

"I am certain of it, and he has told me so, face-to-face, on several occasions. His greatest suffering and the most painful trial of the Latin Church is the crime of pedophile priests, priests who violate their chastity. One only has to read all that he wrote on this subject as a cardinal, then during his pontificate, and, most recently, in *From the Depths of Our Hearts.*

"He never ceased to stress the importance of priestly celibacy for the whole Church. Let me remind you of his words: 'If we separate celibacy from the priesthood, we will no longer see the charismatic character of the priesthood. We will see only a function that the institution itself provides for its own security and needs. If we want to take the priesthood in this light... the Church is no longer understood except as a mere human institution.'"[1]

As a result of the widespread lack of faith on the part of many cardinals, bishops, and priests (many in leadership positions), coupled with the very poor and weak formation of many others, the Church finds itself in a compromised and weakened state more now than ever before. Even so, we can be assured that these evil forces within Holy Mother Church will not prevail; Christ came right out and told us that. It's my understanding that many of the seminaries have cleaned up their act and are once again teaching seminarians the true faith, while emphasizing the important truths of the priesthood. I pray that this is truly the case, because the Church is struggling to heal the wounds caused by the heretics and false teachers that have invaded Her.

Kevin Wells is a devout Christian, a Catholic author and speaker. He was kind enough to write the first guest article on my website christiansmustreunite.com, named after my first book. I requested that he write about the book he had published recently, entitled, *The Priests We Need to Save the Church* (Sophia Institute Press).

Kevin's uncle was Monsignor Thomas Wells, a very holy and good priest, affectionately called "Tommy" by Kevin and the family. Monsignor Wells was a model for many young men entering the priesthood, whom he would mentor. His parishioners, and indeed all Christians, were his main priorities, and he was available to them any time, day or night. A very strong faith and constant prayer sustained this authentic priest.

Kevin tells a chilling story about "Tommy" in the first chapter of his wonderful book. I highly recommend reading this very timely work of love.

As a young man, Kevin Wells was breaking in as a sports-writer for the Tampa Tribune, before eventually becoming a writer for Major League Baseball. In Florida, while attending different Catholic churches, he noticed that some of the priests he came across just didn't have a "light" in their eyes; they were going through the motions, but their parish appeared "dead." He witnessed others who had an obvious love for the Eucharist, and, as a result, that parish was dynamic. The seeds were being planted for the book Kevin would eventually write.

I will now quote pieces of the article he wrote, which appears on my website. Let these words serve as a primer and incentive for you to read his book in its entirety and consider giving one to your priest.

"When my uncle, Msgr. Thomas Wells, was gruesomely murdered in his Mother Seton rectory in 2000, I began to think more about the pastors from those small Florida towns. One of the most joy-filled and impactful priests in the history of Washington, D.C. had that light stolen from his eyes. Satan's work was done; it was accomplished through the large pocket knife of Robert Paul Lucas. After 'Tommy's' death, many hundreds of his former parishioners told my large extended family how he'd changed the course of their lives. He'd saved marriages, redirected suicidal folks, converted atheists, encouraged many men to enter seminaries and ignited groundswells of intentional Catholicism wherever he went for 29 years....

"I sensed Our Lady had been weeping for a very long time. If the Church was ever going to return to what it once was, I thought, it would unfold with the help of the day-to-day witness of the holy and faith-filled parish priest who wanted to be a martyr. The flock would see in him an intentionality, a solemnity, a ferocious zeal to spread the faith, and a deep desire to lead his flock to heaven. With this blazing furnace of truth, there would be sweeping conversions within his parish and world. I was blessed to have several priests as close friends. They've saved marriages, redirected lives and done so much other good work to re-engineer lives because they are men of God attuned to souls....

"I will say that I was greatly urged to write the book by Msgr. John Esseff— once a co-worker of St. Teresa of Calcutta—a renowned exorcist, now 92 years old and still giving retreats and spiritual direction to priests and laity. Many believe he will be a canonized saint in the Church one day. Decades ago, St. Teresa strongly urged Msgr. Esseff to stop working with the poor and turn his attention to the formation of seminarians. Msgr. Esseff reported to me that when he began his work, he found seminaries riddled with homosexuality. This awareness became part of the background and part of the urgency behind my writing. But it was Msgr. Esseff's startling words about priests' prayer that permeated my book: 'We don't have a priest shortage right now, nor do we have a shortage of vocations. What we have is a shortage of priests who pray,' he said. 'We have a severe crisis in our priesthood because priests are not praying. They are not fathers. If we are to do anything well as priests, it must come from prayer, but we've stopped praying. Consequently, most of our priests seem to be bachelors today.'

"Five months into my writing, his words were confirmed when the Theodore McCarrick scandal broke. The ensuing landslide of scandals seemed to prove this staggering lack of supernatural faith among the clergy—still, though, I didn't want to focus on the negatives. I wanted to write a book about the priest that God wanted. The key characteristics I proposed were Eucharistic-centered prayerfulness, asceticism, and a willingness to be radically available to others, and to sacrifice for them. My uncle 'Tommy' was known for walking his neighborhood to chat with people, a chat which regularly included an exhortation to take up one's cross in life, which was softened by his loving and joyful demeanor. I emphasized the Marian self-sacrificing dimension of the priesthood and castigated 'bachelor priests.' I hoped the reader would come to realize that the sacrifices required of a priest are pretty much required of anyone who would be a true follower of Christ. My great hope was that bishops, priests, and seminarians would have the desire, humility, and courage to open themselves to the great challenge I was recommending within. The book was simply a synthesis of what I'd thirsted for from priests for many years.

"At its heart, I was hopeful that the laity might read it, highlight certain passages, and share it with their pastor. At the end of the day, the heart of my book was written for the laity—there is an eight-step process of exceptionalism to help carve us into saints within its pages. For instance, the truest measure of love is Christ nailed to the cross, so we, too, should want to dive into sacrificial living with that same idea of giving ourselves up.

"As Christ and the greatest priest-saints were fervent in prayer, we, too, should have an ardent desire for a devoted and interior prayer life that leads us to true friendship with Christ. If we do these things (and the other characteristics of holy priests described in the book), we'll find ourselves becoming sanctified."²

In the first year of his pontificate, Pope John Paul II composed a letter that went out to all priests in the Catholic Church, which thereafter became an annual custom. He perceived many existing problems and confusions within the Church, and this was written in an attempt to give bishops and priests some direction and clarity. A kind of secularization of many in the priesthood was a particularly important point to make. I will quote parts of what the pope offered in his letter, which was released on Holy Thursday, April 6, 1979:

"...The ministerial priest...forms and rules the priestly people; in the person of Christ, he effects the Eucharistic sacrifice and offers it to God in the name of all the people. The faithful...by virtue of their royal priesthood, participate in the Eucharist. They exercise that priesthood, too, by the reception of the sacraments, prayer and thanksgiving, the witness of a holy life, abnegation and active charity."[3]

At a time when many priests were leaving the priesthood, and others were not conducting themselves in a very priestly manner, Pope John Paul II felt it necessary to emphasize that the "priesthood" of the laity and the consecrated priesthood are infinitely different. The fact that the pope was moved to address a subject that is so fundamental in priestly formation is indicative of the weak teaching that was going on in Catholic seminaries at that time. The Sacrament of Holy Orders effects the ordination of these men, which is imprinted on their very souls. That fact alone makes the discernment and decision to become a priest a serious lifetime commitment for those who feel the call to do so. It is not something that one can just decide to walk away from. Pope John Paul II also had this to say:

"Our sacramental priesthood constitutes a special *ministerium,* that is to say, 'service,' in relation to the community of all believers. It does not however take its origin from that community, as though it were the community that 'called' or 'delegated.' The sacramental priesthood is a gift for that community that comes from Christ, Himself, for the fullness of his priesthood.

"Conscious of this reality, we understand how our priesthood is 'hierarchical,' that is to say connected with the power of forming and governing the priestly people and precisely for this reason 'ministerial.' We carry out this office, through which Christ Himself serves the Father in the work of our salvation. Our priestly existence must be deeply imbued with this service if we wish to effect in an adequate way the Eucharistic sacrifice *in persona Christi*. The priesthood calls for a particular integrity of life and service which is supremely fitting for our priestly identity. It is a question of the humble readiness to accept the gifts of the Holy Spirit and to transmit to others the fruits of love and peace, to give them the certainty of faith from which derives understanding of the meaning of human existence and the capacity to introduce the moral order into the human setting.

"Since the priesthood is given to us so that we can serve others, it cannot be renounced because of the difficulties that we meet and the sacrifices asked of us. Like the apostles, we have left everything to follow Christ; therefore, we must persevere beside Him through the Cross...."[4]

In further differentiating the priesthood from the laity, the saintly pope emphatically stated this:

"Although care for the salvation of others is a task for every member of the people of God, nevertheless, you priests are expected to have a care and commitment which are far greater and different from those of any lay person. This is because your sharing in the priesthood of Jesus Christ differs from theirs 'essentially and not only in degree.'

"The priesthood of Jesus Christ is the first source of care for our salvation. Do not the words, 'the good shepherd is one who lays down his life for his sheep,' refer to the sacrifice of the Cross, the definitive act of Christ's priesthood? Do they not tell priests the road that they must follow? Do they not tell us that our vocation is a singular solicitude for the salvation of our neighbor? That this is the *raison d'etre* of our priestly life, and that only through this solicitude can we find the significance of our life, perfection and holiness? This is taken up in the conciliar decree *Optatam Totius* (8-11, 19-20)."[5]

In a clear and simple manner, the pope went on to say this under the heading "Steward and Witness":

"The priestly life is built on the Sacrament of Orders which imprints on our soul an indelible character. This mark has its 'personalistic' dynamism. The priestly personality must be for others a clear and plain sign and indication. The people want above all to see in us such a sign and indication, and to this they have a right. It may sometimes seem that they do not want this, or that they wish us to be in every way like them. Here one needs a sense of faith and the gift of discernment. It is easy to be guided by appearances and fall victim to a fundamental illusion. Those who call for a secularization of priestly life will undoubtedly abandon us when we succumb to temptation. We shall then cease to be necessary and popular. The only priest who will always prove necessary to the people is the priest who is conscious of the full meaning of his priesthood; who believes profoundly, who prays fervently, who teaches with deep conviction, who puts the Beatitudes into practice in his life, who loves disinterestedly, who is close to everyone, especially to those most in need.

"Our pastoral activity demands that we be close to people and all their problems, but also that we be close to these problems in a priestly way. Only then do we remain ourselves. We must seek truth and justice, the true dimension of which we can only find in Christ. Our task is to serve truth and justice in the perspective of eternal salvation. This salvation takes into account the temporal achievements of the human spirit in the sphere of knowledge and morality, but is not identical with them and goes higher than them. Our brethren in the faith, and unbelievers too, expect us always to be able to show them this perspective, to become real witnesses to it. They expect us to be men of prayer.

"There are those who have united their priestly vocation with an intense life of prayer and penance in the strictly contemplative religious orders. Let them remember that their priestly ministry is ordered to solicitude for the salvation of every human being.

"And this we must remember: It is not lawful for any of us to deserve the the name of 'hireling' of one who, 'since he is not the shepherd and the sheep do not belong to him, abandons the sheep as soon as he sees the wolf coming, and then the wolf attacks and scatters the sheep.' The solicitude of every good shepherd is that all people should have eternal life. May it characterize our personality, and be at the foundation of our priestly identity."[6]

One of the very important things Pope John Paul II instructed all priests is that their priestly formation should not have ended when they left the seminary. In light of the terrible seminaries that have existed in the last half century, that was very wise counsel indeed. The formation of all priests should last a lifetime, just as it should for all Christians. We are all subject to the attitudes, opinions, and machinations in the world, and there is a constant attempt to undermine the Church, to secularize every aspect of our daily lives.

I am of the opinion that we have many, many good and holy priests, but they are human beings that can be influenced by the many different schools of thought that exist in the world. If they don't look at everything through the lens of Catholic teaching and right-ordered morality, they can be led astray. Young, impressionable priests especially need to be careful not to just accept what may turn out to be deceptive concepts and sweet-sounding ideas that they may be presented with. They must always consult the immutable Church teachings when analyzing things that are presented to them by those who may be poorly formed Catholic laity, and even other priests.

The unfortunate fact is that we also have many wayward priests and bishops who are actively promoting heresy and teaching false doctrine to unsuspecting laypeople, and for some reason they are able to do so in an unimpeded manner. In order to restore our Catholic identity, it is important that our priests actually know and understand the true faith and that they teach the truth. We suffer from a severe lack of knowledge on the part of the laity. If one does not understand the faith and Church teaching, it's hard to pass it on to others. A vast number of Catholics actually believe that many of the political and secular beliefs comport with what our Church believes. In many cases, that is absolutely not the case. We must know our faith and study it, and it's the mission of the Catholic priest, on behalf of Christ, to teach us and help keep us in line.

Chapter 17
Champions of the Faith

If we are ever to restore our true Catholic identity and return to the true faith Jesus Christ gave us, we need to decide to fight back against the heresies and false teachers that have infiltrated our Holy Church. When I say "we," I mean good and faithful bishops, priests and, yes, members of the laity. It is my opinion that if devout Catholics study and learn more about the Church and its history, we can help right the many wrongs that have taken place especially in the last half century, although the seeds for the destruction of the Church were planted way before the Vatican II Council occurred. In fact, this evil has been going on in many ways since Judas Iscariot betrayed Our Lord in the Garden of Gethsemane.

In the history of Mother Church, there have been countless heroic individuals who have stepped up to defend her and the immutable teachings Christ gifted to us for our eternal salvation. It seems that now is the time for those of us who want to reclaim our Christian heritage, and the actual truth that runs through it, to speak up and get involved so that the terrible damage that has been done can be repaired. Lest you believe the job is too difficult and hopeless, let's look at the experiences of several Catholic heroes and consider what they went through as they defended the truth. Granted, they are all now recognized as saints by the Church, but it should be the desire of all of us to become saints—in fact, if we make it to heaven, we will be saints.

First, I will mention one of my very favorite saints, Saint Athanasius of Alexandria (also referred to as Athanasius the Great). Because of my admiration for him, I have chosen him to be the patron saint of my apostolate, which arose following my first book, *Christians Must Reunite: Now Is the Time*. My goal is to help people learn more about the Catholic faith—both Catholics and Protestants—in an attempt to bring our separated brethren back to the one, true Church, and to enhance the knowledge of Catholics about their faith. My website can be found at christiansmustreunite.com.

Saint Athanasius was the champion who fought against a heresy that invaded the Church and was embraced by many bishops and priests. This heresy was named Arianism after a presbyter named Arius. The essence of Arianism is that it denied the divinity of Christ. Unbelievably, Arius garnered the support and agreement of several bishops and priests. Athanasius spent 45 years of his life as a bishop, but he was exiled for 17 of those years due to his staunch defense of the true faith. In all, he was exiled five times, but he never took a step back from defending the Holy Trinity. Athanasius was designated a Doctor of the Church in 1568. His winning efforts embodied the very meaning of the word "perseverance."

The Athanasius Creed is somewhat lengthy, but it will give you some insight into how this man viewed the Church, and especially the Trinity. It reads as follows:

"Whoever wishes to be saved must, above all, keep the Catholic faith.

"For unless a person keeps this faith whole and entire, he will undoubtedly be lost forever.

"This is what the Catholic faith teaches: we worship one God in the Trinity and the Trinity in unity.

"We distinguish among the persons, but we do not divide the substance.

"For the Father is a distinct person; the Son is a distinct person; and the Holy Spirit is a distinct person.

"Still the Father and the Son and the Holy Spirit have one divinity, equal glory, and coeternal majesty.

"What the Father is, the Son is, and the Holy Spirit is.

"The Father is uncreated, the Son is uncreated, and the Holy Spirit is uncreated.

"The Father is boundless, the Son is boundless, and the Holy Spirit is boundless.

"The Father is eternal, the Son is eternal, and the Holy Spirit is eternal.

"Nevertheless, there are not three eternal beings, but one eternal being.

"Thus, there are not three uncreated beings, nor three boundless beings, but one uncreated being and one boundless being.

"Likewise, the Father is omnipotent, the Son is omnipotent, and the Holy Spirit is omnipotent.

"Yet, there are not three omnipotent beings, but one omnipotent being.

"Thus, the Father is God, the Son is God, and the Holy Spirit is God.

"But there are not three gods, but one God.

"The Father is Lord, the Son is Lord, and the Holy Spirit is Lord.

"There are not three lords, but one Lord.

"For according to Christian truth, we must profess that each of the persons individually is God; and according to Christian religion we are forbidden to say that there are three gods or lords.

"The Father is not made by anyone, nor created by anyone, nor generated by anyone.

"The Son is not made nor created, but he is generated by the Father alone.

"The Holy Spirit is not made nor created nor generated, but proceeds from the Father and the Son.

"There is, then, one Father, not three Fathers; one Son, but not three sons; one Holy Spirit, not three holy spirits.

"In this Trinity, there is nothing greater, nothing less than anything else. But the entire three persons are coeternal and coequal with one another.

"So that, as we have said, we worship complete unity in the Trinity and the Trinity in unity.

"This, then, is what he who wishes to be saved must believe about the Trinity.

"It is also necessary for eternal salvation that he believes steadfastly in the incarnation of our Lord Jesus Christ.

"The true faith is: we believe and profess that our Lord Jesus Christ, the Son of God, is both God and man.

"He died for our salvation, descended to hell, arose from the dead on the third day.

"He is perfect God; and He is perfect man, with a rational soul and human flesh.

"He is equal to the Father in His divinity, but He is inferior to the Father in His humanity.

"Although He is God and man, He is not two, but one Christ.

"And He is one, not because His divinity was changed into flesh, but because His humanity was assumed to God.

"As a rational soul and flesh are one man, so God and man are one Christ.

"As God He was begotten of the substance of the Father before time; as man He was born in time of the substance of His Mother.

"Ascended into heaven, sits at the right hand of God the Father almighty, and from there He shall come to judge the living and the dead.

"At His coming, all men are to arise with their own bodies; and they are to give an account of their lives.

"Those who have done good deeds will go into eternal life; those who have done evil will go into everlasting fire.

"This is the Catholic faith. Everyone must believe it, firmly and steadfastly; otherwise He cannot be saved.

"Glory be to the Father, and to the Son, and to the Holy Ghost. Amen."

Saint Athanasius the Great prevailed and succeeded in his fight to return the Church and a majority of its bishops and priests to the truth. After years of prayer and his indefatigable efforts, it is evident that God blessed him with abundant graces during his trials and tribulations. The above creed displays the straightforward clarity with which he spoke. That is a trait I try hard to emulate when writing and talking about the Church and its teachings.

Another saint that we Catholics can learn a great deal from is Saint Irenaeus, Bishop of Lyons. He was probably born sometime between AD 115 and 125, but some experts say it could have been a little later. We do know that he was mentored in the faith by Saint Polycarp, who was a disciple of Saint John the Apostle. Many of Irenaeus' writings were against the heresy of Gnosticism. In brief, Gnostics believed that they had an infused, certain knowledge of the mysteries of the universe which made them superior to everyone else. Without going too deep into this mistaken ideology of creation, suffice it to say it was an extreme perversion of Christianity. My purpose here is not to give a history of the different heresies that have appeared over the centuries, but to herald the courageous heroes that have opposed and defeated them. One can find loads of extensive writings on all of the heresies mentioned here if that is desired.

Included in the many great works by Saint Augustine, Bishop of Hippo, was his staunch opposition against the heresy of Pelagianism, named after the theologian Pelagius. The basis of this heresy is that one didn't need divine help when performing good deeds. Augustine believed, along with many others, that we human beings cannot attain true righteousness without the grace of God. Pelagius' mistaken idea posited that people could become self-reliant instead of relying on God's grace in our actions. In other words, if we know the right things to do, we can just do them and attain salvation—without asking Our Lord for help. Pelagianism was finally condemned at the Council of Ephesus in the year AD 431. As far as the Catholic Church was concerned, the matter was closed and Augustine and those who agreed with him were victorious.

Following the Protestant so-called "Reformation," many holy, knowledgeable, and courageous Catholics stood up for the truth of the Church, one of whom was Saint Robert Bellarmine. He is one of the patron saints of catechumens and catechists, which indicates that he knew the faith very well. Bellarmine was a highly regarded cardinal and theologian during his lifetime. In fact, he was tasked with writing two catechisms on behalf of Pope Clement VIII, who regarded him as one of the premier Catholic minds within the Church. His work in refuting the Protestant heresy was very edifying for Catholics who might have been questioning their Church and considering converting to Protestantism.

Another distortion of Christianity arose within the sphere of Protestantism, which was called Calvinism. The promoter of this version was one John Calvin. As we know, Protestantism has now blossomed into over 30,000 separate denominations, each with different beliefs and interpretations of Christianity and Scripture. When Calvinism was spreading and was dominant in Geneva, there was a Catholic bishop named Francis de Sales, who singlehandedly won thousands back to the one, true Church. It is said that he held Holy Mass in secret many times, where he convinced many that Calvinism was not the way to go. He would even prepare pamphlets on Catholicism and slip them under the doors of people who may have left the faith, possibly inviting them to one of his Masses. Saint Francis de Sales deserves our sincere gratitude for his defense of the Catholic Church.

Saint Thomas Aquinas wrote an extensive work containing everything and anything pertaining to Catholic theology. He called it the *Summa Theologiae*, also known as *Summa*

Theologica. It is voluminous to be sure, made up of five volumes that are worth their weight in gold. In my opinion, Saint Thomas Aquinas was a supercharged apologist for Catholic doctrine; he left no stone unturned. It was written from 1265-1274, and the first completed printed edition was in 1485. He wrote the *Summa* for seminarians, theologians, and educated laity. Within the pages, he refutes heresies, myths, and misconceptions about Catholic teaching. This important work has been frequently quoted by popes and bishops in their writings and teachings over the centuries. Saint Thomas Aquinas' *Summa* was especially important at that time in history because Islam was on the rise. Many consider this holy man to be the greatest Catholic theologian that has ever lived.

I have now presented to you a brief list of exceptional men that have done great things for Christ's Holy Catholic Church. It is very important to note at this point that we in the laity are meant to do as they have done. Christ's Great Commission to "Go, therefore, and make disciples of all nations..." (Matthew 28:19) was meant for all of us, not just the Apostles.

Archbishop Fulton Sheen said these famous words:

"Who's going to save our Church? It's not our bishops, it's not our priests and it's not the religious. It is up to you, the people. You have the minds, the eyes and the ears to save the Church. Your mission is to see that the priests act like priests, your bishops act like bishops, and the religious act like religious."

In order to defend and fight for Christ's Church, we must first understand what it is we are fighting for. As Catholics, we need to study and learn anew the teachings of the Church; otherwise, our foundation is weak and we are uninformed. We must stop the heretical programs that wayward parishes are offering to unsuspecting Catholics who may not know the faith well. We must fight against the heretical priests and bishops who are trying to change the Church to their personal liking. We must insist on homosexuality being rooted out of seminaries and oppose priests who preach tolerance for the LBGTQ community from the pulpit. It is incumbent upon us to oppose sinfulness in all its forms, including the mistaken idea that we are uncharitable homophobes if we oppose the gay lifestyle.

Because of the extremely weak catechesis that has occurred in the last half century, our Church has been stained and the truth has been hidden from us by bishops and priests with hidden agendas. We have been manipulated by a Church hierarchy that, unbelievably, seeks to make the Church into some kind of a nice-sounding, feel-good institution where almost anything goes.

We, the good bishops, priests, and laity, have the capability of saving the Church in our time, and hopefully repairing the damage that has been done over such a long period of time. It's time for the laity to step up in support of our good and holy bishops and priests, but to oppose the bad ones. If we work hard and are not afraid to speak up for Mother Church, we can do great things just like the saints of old. More and more lay apostolates are rising up to defend the truth, and they seem to be having a positive effect. We need to hold to account those who seek to deceive us and make the Church something it was never meant to be.

We need to be brave in the face of being called uncharitable, unmerciful, judgmental, homophobic, and all the other epithets and insults that faithful, traditional Catholics now face from the "let's just be nice" crowd. Yes, we are taught to love all human beings, but we are also taught to oppose sin in all its forms. If we love others in true charity and mercy, we have nothing to be ashamed of. We should adhere to the Word of God and not buckle to the words of men.

I wrote this book to make the case that we must band together as brothers and sisters in Christ to restore our Catholic identity. I hope and pray that I have contributed to making this happen.

Notes

Chapter One

1. Villarrubia, Elenore. "Bella Dodd—From Communist to Catholic," Catholicism.org, August 31, 2010, https://catholicism.org/bella-dodd-%E2%80%94-from-communist-to-catholic.html.

2. Marshall, Taylor R. *Infiltration: The Plot to Destroy the Church from Within*. Manchester, NH: Sophia Institute Press, 2019.

3. Ibid. (Foreword by Bishop Athanasius Schneider.)

4. Schneider, Bishop Athanasius. *Christus Vincit: Christ's Triumph Over the Darkness of the Age*. Brooklyn: NY: Angelico Press, 2019.

5. Gray, David L. *The Catholic Catechism on Freemasonry*. Belleville, IL: Saint Dominic's Media, 2020.

6. Ibid.

Chapter Two

1. Pew Research Center. "What Americans Know About Religion," July, 23, 2019, https://www.pewforum.org/2019/07/23/what-americans-know-about-religion/.

Chapter Three

1. Rossini, Connie. *Is Centering Prayer Catholic?* Omaha, NE: Four Waters Press, 2015.

Chapter Four

1. Benkovic, Johnnette S. *The New Age Counterfeit.* California: Queenship Publishing, 1993.

2. Brinkmann, Susan. *Learn to Discern Compendium: Is it Christian or New Age?* Oldsmar, FL: Simon Peter Press, 2015.

3. Kephart, Rick. "Enneagram Versus the Catholic Church," EWTN, 1994, https://www.ewtn.com/catholicism/library/enneagram-versus-the-catholic-church-6070.

4. Pacwa, Mitch, S.J. *Catholics and the New Age.* Ohio: Servant Books, 1992.

5. Locke, Laura. "The Dangers of Reiki," Catholic Answers, November 1, 2012, https://www.catholic.com/magazine/print-edition/the-dangers-of-reiki.

Chapter Five

1. Likoudis, Paul. "Jung Replaces Jesus in Catholic Spirituality," article in The Wanderer, St. Paul, MN, 1995.

2. Thevathasan, Pravin. "Carl Jung's Journey from God," Catholic Culture, May 15, 2003, https://www.catholicculture.org/culture/library/view.cfm?recnum=4676.

3. Hichborn, Michael. "Dissident priests to boost homosexuality in Santa Fe diocese; archbishop silent," LifesiteNews website, June 18, 2018, https://www.lifesitenews.com/opinion/dissident-priests-to-boost-homosexuality-in-santa-fe-diocese-archbishop-sil.

Chapter Seven

1. Dolan, Greg. "Why Can't the Middle Class Afford Catholic School Anymore?" Education Next, August 15, 2018, https://www.educationnext.org/why-cant-middle-class-afford-catholic-school-anymore/.

Chapter Eight

1. Aquinas, St. Thomas. *Summa Theologica,* Third Part, Question 82, Article 3.

2. Schneider, Bishop Athanasius. *Dominus Est—It Is the Lord!* Pine Beach, NJ: Newman House Press, 2008.

3. *Vulgate.* When the disciples recognized the risen Lord— *Dominus est* (John 21:7).

Chapter Nine

1. Van der Lande, Gillian. "Should ALPHA Be Used in a Catholic Context?" Our Lady's Warriors, 1999, https://www.ourladyswarriors.org/dissent/alpha1.htm.

Chapter Ten

1. Rose, Michael S. *Ugly As Sin.* Manchester, NH: Sophia Institute Press, 2001.

2. Ibid.

3. Ibid.

Chapter Eleven

1. Thigpen, Paul. *The Rapture Trap*. West Chester, PA: Ascension Press, 2002.

Chapter Twelve

1. *Precis of Official Catholic Teaching on Marriage, Family, and Sexuality*. Volume IV, page 98. Silver Spring, MD: CCSP, 1994.

2. Ibid., 99.

3. Ibid., 99.

4. Ibid., 100-101.

5. Ibid., 103-104.

6. Ibid., 107.

7. Ibid., 123.

8. Ibid., 125.

9. Ibid., 127.

10. Ibid., 127-128.

11. Ibid., 128.

12. Ibid., 140-142.

Chapter Thirteen

1. Busenitz, Nathan. "The Gift of Tongues: Comparing the Church Fathers with Contemporary Pentecostalism*," The Master's Seminary Journal* 17, no. 1, (Spring 2006): 61-78, https://tms.edu/m/Busenitz-2006-vol-17-no-1-1-18.pdf.

2. Ibid.

3. Ibid.

Chapter Fifteen

1. *Precis of Official Catholic Teaching on the Sanctity of Human Life.* Volume V, 10-11. Silver Spring, MD: CCSP, 1994.

2. Ibid., 11.

3. Ibid., 48.

4. Ibid., 50.

5. Ibid., 51.

6. Ibid., 60.

7. Ibid., 61-62.

Chapter Sixteen

1. Pentin, Edward. "Cardinal Sarah: The Priesthood Today 'Is in Mortal Danger,'" National Catholic Register, February 8, 2020, https://www.ncregister.com/interview/cardinal-sarah-the-priesthood-today-is-in-mortal-danger.

2. Wells, Kevin. "The Priests We Need," Christians Must Reunite, May 13, 2020, https://christiansmustreunite.com/blog/priests-we-need.

3. *Precis of Official Catholic Teaching on the Ordained Priesthood.* Volume VII, 179-180. Silver Spring, MD: CCSP, 1994.

4. Ibid., 180.

5. Ibid., 180.

6. Ibid., 181-182.

About the Author

Paul A. Nelson converted to the Catholic Church at the age of sixteen. His faith journey included leaving the Church temporarily. While attending a Baptist church, he had a life-changing experience which eventually led him to return to the Catholic Church.

Nelson embarked on a deep personal study of Christianity that lasted for many years, after which he studied the catechetical coursework developed by the late Servant of God Father John Hardon, founder of the Marian Catechist Apostolate, and became a Consecrated Marian Catechist. His first book, *Christians Must Reunite: Now Is the Time,* was released in 2019.

Nelson's primary focus is his faith, his family, and teaching the truth about Christ and the Catholic Church.

https://christiansmustreunite.com/

Christians Must Reunite: Now Is the Time
by Paul A. Nelson

Paul A. Nelson

We live in a secular culture where, unbelievably, speaking the truth is politically incorrect. Political philosophies now govern the thinking of people, many in direct contradiction to what the Church teaches. Christianity is being minimized more every day, and perverse ideas regarding marriage, gender, mercy, and other things are becoming normalized and accepted.

There is a tremendous need today for clarity and truth. We cannot each have our own "truth," as many seem to think. Christ is the Truth, and His Church is the Truth, and the Bible is the Truth.

Within *Christians Must Reunite*, you will find clear, concise, and accurate teaching. If you are seeking the truth, you will find theologically correct, to-the-point, and loving words on these pages. It's time to stop dancing around the issues.

Take the eye-opening journey through this short work of love. You won't be disappointed.

Scan this code with a smartphone:

Available at https://leoninepublishers.com/bookstore

About Leonine Publishers

Leonine Publishers LLC makes fine Catholic literature available to Catholics throughout the English-speaking world. Leonine Publishers offers an innovative "hybrid" approach to book publication that helps authors as well as readers. Please visit our web site to learn more about us. Browse our online bookstore to find more solid Catholic titles to uplift, challenge, and inspire.

Our patron and namesake is Pope Leo XIII, a prudent, yet uncompromising pope during the stormy years at the close of the 19th century. Please join us as we ask his intercession for our family of readers and authors.

www.leoninepublishers.com

CPSIA information can be obtained
at www.ICGtesting.com
Printed in the USA
JSHW020002220423
40698JS00002B/155